T0150978

INSIGHT ⊙ GUIDES

EXPLORE

COSTA RICA

⊙ Walking Eye App

HOW THE EBOOKS WORK

The eBooks are provided in EPUB file format. Please note that you will need an eBook reader installed on your device to open the file. Many devices come with this as standard, but you may still need to install one manually from Google Play.

The eBook content is identical to the content in the printed guide.

HOW TO DOWNLOAD THE WALKING EYE APP

1. Download the Walking Eye App from the App Store or Google Play.
2. Open the app and select the scanning function from the main menu.
3. Scan the QR code on this page – you will then be asked a security question to verify ownership of the book.
4. Once this has been verified, you will see your eBook in the purchased ebook section, where you will be able to download it.

Other destination apps and eBooks are available for purchase separately or are free with the purchase of the Insight Guide book.

CONTENTS

AWAY FROM IT ALL

Go off grid at an eco-lodge on the Osa Peninsula or a castaway lodge across the Golfo Dulce (route 8). Pamper yourself at a hot springs spa in Arenal (route 9) or relax with yoga and therapeutic massage in Nosara (route 11).

RECOMMENDED ROUTES FOR...

CHILDREN

Introduce youngsters to endearing baby sloths at the Sloth Sanctuary in Cahuita (route 12) and remarkable bats at the Bat Jungle in Monteverde (route 10). Enjoy a beach vacation in family-friendly Sámara (route 11).

FOODIES

Savor San José's eclectic downtown restaurant scene (route 1) and get a taste for spicy Caribbean cuisine in Cahuita (route 12). Nosara has healthy, organic offerings and Sámara has two of the country's standout Italian restaurants (route 11).

HISTORY AND CULTURE

Explore pre-Columbian culture at San José's Gold or Jade museums (route 1) and at the Finca 6 Museum of the Spheres (route 7). Vestiges of colonial times survive in the Orosí Valley (route 3) and Heredia (route 2).

OUTDOOR ADVENTURE

Hike in the highland Cloudbridge Reserve (route 5), zip-line through lowland rain forest at Hacienda Barú (route 7), learn to surf in Nosara (route 11) and snorkel Punta Uva's coral reef (route 12).

TROPICAL NATURE

Take a walk in Monteverde's cloud forest (route 10), visit Wilson Botanical Garden's world-famous collection of heliconias (route 6), or take a boat through Central America's largest mangrove (route 7).

VIEWS

Take in idyllic views of the Orosí Valley (route 3) and of the Arenal Volcano rising above misty Lake Arenal (route 9). Embrace picture-perfect Playa Carrillo (route 11) and spectacular sunsets on Dominicalito Beach (route 7).

WILDLIFE

Seek the resplendent quetzal in the highlands (route 4); watch snakes being fed a live lunch (route 7); see butterflies emerge from cocoons (routes 9 and 10); or glimpse a secretive tapir or jaguar in Corcovado (route 8).

INTRODUCTION

An introduction to Costa Rica's geography, customs, and culture, plus illuminating background information on cuisine, history, and what to do when you're there.

Fisherman mending his net, Puntarenas

EXPLORE COSTA RICA

With an astonishing array of natural habitats, exotic flora and fauna, and miles of pristine coastline, Costa Rica is a magnet for nature-lovers. Outdoor adventures and off-the-grid experiences abound, within a sustainable framework of genuine ecotourism.

From impoverished, neglected Spanish colony to progressive, democratic republic, Costa Rica has made some wise public policy decisions along the way. Among them was the creation in 1955 of the first national park, protecting Poás Volcano, which set the country on a conservation course that has made it one of the world's premier ecotourism destinations.

GEOGRAPHY AND LAYOUT

Wedged between Nicaragua and Panama on the Central America isthmus, Costa Rica stretches between 8 and 11 degrees above the equator. With a land area of just 51,000 sq km (20,000 sq miles), Costa Rica extends only 460km (286 miles) from top to bottom, and at its narrowest point, measures 120km (74.5 miles) across.

Small as it is, four mountain ranges, which separate east from west, present challenges in traveling around the country. Two-lane, winding roads have to climb up and over mountains, and snake along indented coastlines.

There is no countrywide train service, but buses are plentiful and relatively cheap. Many remote destinations are reachable only by boat or small plane. To get to some of the off-the-beaten routes described in this book, driving a car, preferably with four-wheel drive and a good navigation system, is the best option.

HISTORY

Since the army was abolished in 1949, governments have devoted a large percentage of the country's resources to education, health, and conservation. The resulting social peace has made Costa Rica a relatively safe and pleasant place to visit.

The investment in conservation has paid off, too. Almost a quarter of the country is now protected in national parks, biological preserves, wildlife refuges, and private preserves, home to more than 900 species of birds, 250 mammals, and almost 6 percent of the world's total identified species.

CLIMATE

Although it's so close to the equator, the climate is surprisingly varia-

White-faced capuchin

Pre-Columbian model display, Jade Museum, San José

ble and moderate, thanks to changes in altitude. In the high central valley, where most of the population lives, it's 'perennial springtime,' with average temperatures ranging from 20°C to 26°C (68°F to 78°F) day and night. Higher up in the mountains, temperatures at night can fall into the low teens Celsius (50s Fahrenheit). Down on both coasts, however, temperatures are decidedly tropical, with very high humidity and temperatures climbing into the 30s Celsius (90s, Fahrenheit).

A bushmaster, the largest New World snake

The country's two seasons, *invierno* (winter) and *verano* (summer) are more related to rainfall than changes in temperature. The rainy season (*invierno*) starts in mid-May and runs through the end of November. But even in the rainy season, mornings are often dry and sunny, followed by heavy afternoon downpours.

Generally speaking, high season in Costa Rica is December through the end of March, with a second burst of tourism May to September. Toward the end of the rainy season can be the most pleasant time to visit since the landscape is at its lushest and greenest, and the sun-seeking crowds from northern climates have not yet arrived.

POPULATION

The latest census puts the population at just under 5 million. The overwhelming majority of *Ticos,* as they call themselves, are of mostly Spanish heritage, with various mixtures of *mestizo* (indigenous) and other European ancestry. The vast majority – around 70 percent – live in the Central Valley.

The country's largest minority is the English-speaking, Afro-American population on the Caribbean coast, descendant of Jamaican immigrants. A sizeable population of Chinese (called Chinos) is descended from 19th-century indentured laborers.

Mercado Central, San José

As in many Spanish colonies, the conquistadors almost obliterated the indigenous population, through disease and brutality. Today, that population is estimated to be 100,000, divided into distinctive linguistic groups, living in remote preserves and villages around the country.

In the 20th century, the natural beauty and easy pace of life converted many tourists, from the US, Canada, Great Britain, and Europe, into permanent residents.

The largest immigration wave occurred during and after the 1980s Nicaraguan Civil War, which spurred an exodus of thousands of Nicaraguans seeking refuge in Costa Rica. *Nicos*, as Ticos call them, have not been universally welcomed, but many are providing essential services in low-paying jobs and working their way up.

Along with permanent residents and undocumented workers, more than 2 million visitors arrive each year, swelling the local population.

LOCAL CUSTOMS

The first thing most visitors notice is how polite and friendly Ticos are. Costa Rica is the epitome of a 'kind and gentle' society. Away from the larger towns and the busy capital city, people still smile, nod, and say *Buenos Dias* or *Adíos*, even to passing strangers.

Family life is still the main focus here and family roots are deep and wide, with the same surnames repeating around the country. Most extended families retain close links with their rural past, spending many weekends and most vacations at family *fincas* (farm properties).

In San José and most tourist destinations, English is widely spoken. Children study English throughout their school years, so young people are the most likely to speak English, or at least understand enough English to help you out.

A helpful sign around Arenal Volcano

Fun on the swings, Tortuguero

'*Tranquilo*' (stay calm) and *Pura Vida* (pure life!) still rule in Costa Rica, where the pace of life, even in the bustling capital city, is relatively laid back. But don't expect things to happen fast or always efficiently. Another important watchword to learn is *ahorita*, which literally translates as 'in a little while,' but can stretch into hours or even days.

Most government and business offices close from noon to 2pm, but museums generally stay open. Many banks close early in the afternoon on weekdays, around 3pm, but some are open even on Saturdays, and there are ATMs almost everywhere. Sunday used to be a sacrosanct family day, but more and more shopping malls and grocery stores are open all day Sunday now.

Since the sun rises between 5 and 5.30am, the day starts early in Costa Rica. With sundown around 6pm, year round, night closes in quickly. Except in the cities and tourist hubs, you won't find restaurants open or much in the way of nightlife after 8 or 9pm. The night owls here are mostly of the avian species.

DON'T LEAVE COSTA RICA WITHOUT...

Savoring a breakfast à la Tico. Sit down to at least one *típico* breakfast of *gallo pinto*, tortillas, *queso*, and tortillas with *natilla*. La Criollita in San José is an excellent place to have breakfast (see page 35).

Flying through the air. Zip-lining is a thrilling way to experience Costa Rica's rain forest. Wing Nuts Canopy Tour in Sámara is adept at calming the most apprehensive youngsters and oldsters (see page 96). The Osa Canopy Tour, more challenging, will suit the more adventurous (see page 70).

Watching a Pacific sunset. With or without a tropical drink in hand, join locals and visitors on Playa Pelades in Nosara in the daily ritual of watching the sun set over the Pacific Ocean. Look out for the fabled green flash as the sun

disappears under the horizon (see page 94).

Climbing a volcano. Get up-close and personal with Arenal Volcano by hiking up the steep Lava Trail (see page 82).

Watching a butterfly take wing. Of all the wild things in Costa Rica, butterflies are the easiest to see and the most captivating. Watch one emerge from its cocoon and release it with your own hands into the Butterfly Garden in Monteverde (see page 87).

Going off grid. The greatest luxury in Costa Rica is escaping the noise of modern civilization. The last outpost is the Osa Peninsula where you can walk the scenic Coastal Path from Drake Bay (see page 69), or wander the forest preserves of the eco-lodges along the road to Carate (see page 76).

POLITICS AND ECONOMICS

Throughout its history, the political pendulum in Costa Rica has swung between conservatives upholding religious and business interests, to socialists fighting for progressive social programs and tolerance.

The current president, Luis Solís, heads the Citizens' Action Party. He was elected on a left-of-center platform of rooting out corruption, revamping the country's infrastructure, and shoring up public health care and the social security systems. His job has been made difficult by a fractious legislature that can hardly agree on anything. Some economic setbacks have also played a part, including the loss of 1,500 jobs when US-owned Intel closed down its microchip manufacturing plant.

Agricultural exports – pineapple, coffee, and bananas – are still an important sector of the economy, but other high-tech industries, such as the manufacture of medical devices, are coming to the fore. With a huge supply of well-educated, bilingual young people, customer-service call centers are big business here and are catapulting many young people into a new, prosperous middle class.

High-rises are sprouting all around San José and its prosperous suburbs, along with mega-shopping malls, multiplex movie theaters, and outposts of upscale international restaurants. But for all the contemporary glitz, outside the city, Costa Rica is still a developing country with – for the most part – basic infrastructure with a polished veneer.

And that is its real charm and appeal. You can expect a well-organized, civil, safe environment, complete with high-speed Internet and cell phones. But what you really come to experience lies beyond the city limits.

Tourism is now one of the country's leading industries. With its dense jungles, impressive volcanoes, abundant wildlife, and pristine beaches, Costa Rica has all the necessary natural ingredients. What sets it apart from

Costa Rican coffee is rated among the best in the world

Scarlet macaw flying over the rain forest

other nature-friendly destinations, is the focus on sustainable ecotourism. And nowhere else in Central America will visitors find the high quality of this country's trained and licensed nat-uralist guides. Wherever you travel, you will find bilingual guides who can add a lot of value to your trip with their expertise.

Bienvenido and *pura vida*!

TOP TIPS FOR VISITING COSTA RICA

Hire a naturalist guide. Tropical forests present an inscrutable green wall of vegetation. Expert guides know where to look. Follow the naturalist guides at Hacienda Barú on a walk in the lowland Pacific rain forest (see page 66). Or sign up for a birding tour with a Paraíso Quetzal bird guide high up on Cerro de la Muerte (see page 50).

Walk, don't talk, on forest trails. To spot wildlife, you'll need to walk softly and stay as quiet as possible. 'Walk, don't look,' and 'Look, don't walk' will keep you from standing in the path of an army-ant column or tripping over a root whilst taking aim with binoculars or camera.

Pack essential gear. Binoculars are a must for catching close-ups of birds and animals. A light daypack allows you to be hands-free. A reusable, easy-to-clean water bottle is essential, as is a head-lamp for night tours or reading in bed.

Sun and bug protection. Bring plenty of sunscreen and insect repellent. Anti-itch cream will soothe the bites you do get. You also need a wide-brimmed sun hat. A baseball cap won't keep equatorial sun from burning your neck and ears. Sandals won't do on a forest trail, where

your feet can be exposed to biting ants. **It's called the rain forest for a reason.** Bring a light, foldable poncho or rain-proof jacket, plus plenty of socks and waterproof hiking shoes.

Stay healthy. Bring prescription drugs in their original containers, along with any over-the-counter medicines you may not be able to find easily in Costa Rica. Pack your favorite cosmetics and toiletries in small, travel-size containers.

Don't make yourself an easy target. No need to be paranoid, but leave jew-elry and expensive watches back home. Carry only as much cash as you need on each outing. Make a copy of your passport ID and stamped date of entry pages to carry with you; leave your pass-port and extra credit cards in the hotel safe. Don't leave valuables in your car or unattended on the beach and don't hang backpacks, bags, or purses over chair backs.

Don't hurry, be happy. It's impossible to overestimate how long it will take to drive from one place to the next. Heavy trucks, traffic jams and road works, and getting lost can all slow you down, so give yourself lots of time to enjoy the scenery.

Cooking up some street fare

FOOD AND DRINK

Costa Rican cuisine used to suffer from the monotony of rice and beans, but international restaurants and creative local chefs using exotic local ingredients are now making eating in Costa Rica an adventure in itself. Buen provecho!

Traditional Costa Rican cuisine may never make a gourmand's 'best of' list. It can be a little bland, relying heavily on cooked rice and beans, vegetables, fish, beef, chicken, and seafood.

But that perception is slowly changing, given the new worldwide concern with healthy, low-fat, organically sourced food. And Costa Rica's traditional diet ticks almost every box for health-conscious visitors. Along with an influx of restaurants featuring international cuisines, local chefs are updating and fine-tuning Costa Rican specialties, creating a more cosmopolitan dining scene across the country. Organic markets are also popping up, selling local vegetables, fruits, and cheeses.

LOCAL CUISINE

Rice and beans are part of almost all *comida típica* (typical food). Bowls of each will appear on the table at just about every meal in a Tico household or restaurant.

Most Costa Ricans do not like spicy food. The most common spices are salt, black pepper, onion, garlic, cilantro (fresh coriander), and mild chili pepper. A dash of Salsa Lizano, a local fruitier version of Worcestershire sauce, perks up flavors and is usually found on the table, along with spicier *chilero* or Tabasco sauce.

Typical dishes

The classic Costa Rican breakfast dish is *gallo pinto* (literally, painted rooster), a mix of rice and black or red beans, flavored with onion, cilantro, garlic, and finely chopped bell peppers. It's usually served with scrambled or fried eggs, a slice of fried, soft Turrialba cheese, warm corn tortillas, and a dab of *natilla* (sour cream). Cooked well, and enlivened with a dash of Salsa Lizano, it's a filling and flavorful start to any day. In rural areas, you'll also see it served at every meal, minus the eggs.

A typical lunchtime offering is *casado* (literally, husband), named for the daily fare a man expects to receive after he marries. This is a hearty meal that might include any or all of the following: rice, beans, cabbage salad, spaghetti, French fries, pan-fried or sauced chicken, pork, fish, or beef. To sweeten up the meal, there's often a chunk of fried, sweet plantain as well.

The quintessential Sunday family lunch is either *arroz con pollo*, rice sautéed with shredded chicken, diced onions, peppers,

Ceviche – raw fish marinated in lemon juice

carrots, and peas or green beans. Another traditional favorite is *olla de carne*, a slow-cooked stew with root and green vegetables, flavored with beef broth and chunks of less expensive cuts of beef.

On the lighter side

For a lighter lunch, order a ceviche, small cubes of fresh white fish, shrimp, and other shellfish marinated in lime juice and olive oil, fresh cilantro, onions, and bell peppers for at least 12 hours. It's served with salty crackers or rounds of cooked green plantain.

Traditional salads consist of shredded purple and green cabbage and carrots, bathed in a very vinegary dressing. But leafier vegetables and tomatoes are becoming more available, and salads are beginning to become more interesting.

Dessert often features rice, again, this time in creamy, cinnamon-flavored *arroz con leche* (rice pudding), studded with plump raisins. Another favorite is *Tres leches*, a three-layer pudding cake made with three milks: two-percent, evaporated, and sweetened condensed. Caramel or coconut flans feature also on most menus.

Specialties

Small as it is, Costa Rica does have distinctive regional specialties.

On the Caribbean coast, African and West Indian influences show up in hotter spices and the generous use of coconut oil and milk. Yams and breadfruit take the place of potatoes. Rice here is cooked in a pot filled with red beans, coconut milk, and aromatic herbs. Another specialty, which is getting harder to find, is spicy *rondón*, a slow-cooked fish and root vegetable stew flavored with curry.

In Guanacaste, pre-Columbian traditions persist in the large variety of corn-based dishes, both savory and sweet.

On the Pacific coast, Puntarenas specializes in shellfish, including *guiso de cambute* (conch stew) and *chuchecas* (black clams) sautéed in butter and garlic. Shrimp abound, but there is considerable environmental concern over the shrimp boats' destructive bottom-dredging methods, which disrupt the marine food chain.

A more ecological seafood delicacy is the oysters farmed on the Nicoya Peninsula and shipped the same day to seafood restaurants as far away as San José.

Vegetarian and gluten-free fare

Minus the meat or fish, vegetarians and vegans can eat very well in Costa Rica. You can order a *casado* without the ani-

---

Nouvelle cuisine

Costa Rican nouvelle cuisine may sound like a contradiction in terms, but local chefs are creating new recipes, rewriting traditional ones, and adding local flavors to international recipes to create a tropical fusion. Watch for dishes like *crema de pejibaye*, a delicate, creamy soup made from peach palm fruits, long a staple of indigenous Amerindians.

Refreshing watermelon juice

mal protein or try a *sopa negra* made with black beans, onions, and cilantro, with or without hard-boiled eggs floating on top.

Gluten-sensitive travelers can fill up on fruit, vegetables, and rice and enjoy just about every *comida típica* dish. The abundance of corn dishes – *tortillas, tamales,* and *chorreadas* (cheese-flavored tortillas) – replaces any need for wheat. There's even sweet *tamal de elote,* a sweet, solid corn pudding, to take the place of cake.

TROPICAL FRUITS

The sheer variety of fruits on offer at markets and roadside stands is staggering. You may encounter fruits you have never heard of before, since many are never exported. Along with familiar but fresher and tastier pineapples, mangoes, papaya, and passion fruit, look for *mora* (blackberry), *carambola* (star fruit), *guanabana* (soursop), *sapodilla* (naseberry), and *maman chino* (rambutan). Nothing beats a perfectly ripe Costa Rican banana. It's creamier and more flavorful than any exported banana you have ever tasted.

North Americans and Europeans are enjoying the health benefits of tropical fruits more and more. One US health food chain sells tiny papaya pills and touts juice made from *noni* fruits, common on the Caribbean coast, as a health tonic.

WHERE TO EAT

In San José, you are spoiled for choice when it comes to trendy, international res-

taurants. Italian, Spanish, Asian, French, Peruvian, and American-style restaurants abound. Notable among San José's world-class restaurants are Grano de Oro, in an elegant mansion (see page 118), and Park Café (see page 119) owned by a Michelin-starred British chef.

Many of the newer, sophisticated restaurants are packed into the upscale western suburbs of Escazú and Santa Ana. The major tourist hubs and luxury resorts also offer high-priced fine international restaurants, along with less expensive ethnic eateries.

Eating like the locals

Throughout the country, you'll find *comida típica* at inexpensive *sodas* (casual, small cafés), as well as in covered markets and weekly open-air street markets. Cevicherías serve up seafood in just about every town, with the best located on both coasts. *Chicharronías,* serving tender *chicharróns* (chunks of rendered pork and deep-fried pigskin), are popular among meat-eaters.

Across the country, you'll also find endless pizza parlors, serving up varying styles of what Ticos believe pizza to be, along with Chinese restaurants specializing in Tico-style *comida china.*

DRINKS

Most water in built-up areas and tourist towns is perfectly safe to drink. Bottled water is available everywhere, but in the interests of sustainability, tour-

Gallo pinto, a classic

A roadside fruit stall

ists are encouraged to carry refillable water containers.

Refreshing fruit elixirs

Many of the country's exotic fruits are processed into pulp and mixed with water to make *refrescos naturales*. Mixed with milk, they make delicious, thick *batidos* (fruity milkshakes). Commercial bottled fruit drinks are on sale everywhere, but they cannot match a *naturale* made with fresh fruit pulp and your specified amount of sugar.

In the land of coffee

Coffee, of course, is the nation's signature beverage. You can buy the best, high-altitude Arabic coffee in the world, *molido* (ground) or *grano entero* (whole beans), but, surprisingly, you have to look hard to find coffee made properly.

In the past, big metal pots of coffee mixed with milk and sugar simmered away on stovetops in local *sodas*. A metal ladle or cup was used to scoop out each serving. At home, coffee was made the old-fashioned way, with a *chorreador*, a wooden stand with a cheese-cloth 'sock' in which ground coffee was placed, and hot water slowly poured over.

Spurred on by coffee growers, such as Coopedota and Britt, there's a new emphasis on training baristas and introducing the fine art of espresso-making. Cafés serving European-style coffee are now springing up across the country.

Cool brews

On the alcoholic side, ice-cold beer is very popular in Costa Rica. The Cervecería Costa Rica holds a monopoly on brewing versions of international beers. Imperial lager is the most popular, followed by local versions of Pilsen and Bavaria.

Craft beers and microbreweries are popping up all over the country, incorporating tropical flavors into very different styles of beer. Craft beer pub-crawl tours are now offered in San José.

There are no wineries in Costa Rica – the climate does not support grape growing. The majority of wines sold and served in restaurants come from Chile and Argentina. More expensive French, Italian, and Spanish wines are available in upscale grocery stores, such as Auto Mercado, and in high-end restaurants at a high price.

Cocktail time

Guaro, distilled from sugar cane, is the inexpensive, high-potency alcohol of choice. Cocktails, especially in tourist spots and resort hotels, are wildly popular, with rum, tequila, and vodka cocktails taking on tropical-fruit flavors.

Food and Drink Prices

Prices for a main dish with a local (non-imported) beverage.
$ = under $10
$$ = $10–15
$$$ = $15–20
$$$$ = over $20

SHOPPING

From the days of tacky miniature painted ox-carts and frog-shaped fridge magnets, Costa Rica's souvenirs are becoming ever more sophisticated. There is now an array of high-quality indigenous crafts and artisanal wood and textile items to tempt you.

Most visitors do not come to Costa Rica to shop. Mega-shopping malls here contain the same retail chains that encircle the globe, often charging higher prices than you would likely pay at home. Open-air markets sell local crafts in every tourist destination and itinerant peddlers selling jewelry made of seeds and shells scour the beaches for buyers.

There are a few large-scale souvenir emporiums spread around the country, concentrated in heavily touristed areas. The town of Sarchí, northwest of San José, is famous for its intricately painted ox-carts, both full-size and miniature, and for handmade furniture. Leather-and-wood rocking chairs are often shipped abroad.

Some of the best souvenirs can be found in San José museums. Look for replica pre-Columbian gold jewelry at the Gold Museum; and jade jewelry and figurines at the Jade Museum.

LOCAL CRAFTS

Indigenous crafts

If you're interested in indigenous cultures, the best buys are intricately carved and painted wooden masks made by the Boruca indigenous group: cotton purses, tote bags, and hats hand-woven and colored with natural dyes; small *netsuke*-like figures and jewelry carved out of *tagua* nut (vegetable ivory); and ornately embroidered cotton dresses from the Guaymí indigenous group.

If you don't come across these items on your travels, check out Galeria Namú (Avenida 7 between calles 5 and 7; tel: 2256-3412; https://galerianamu.com) in downtown San José. This shop has the largest range of authentic indigenous crafts, including many museum-quality pieces.

Artisanal wood

Bowls, cutting boards, placemats, and boxes made from tropical hardwoods are sold everywhere. The finest quality boxes and bowls, lathed from seasoned woods and polished to satin-smooth finish, are more expensive but exquisite. Look for woodcrafts with the name Barry Biesanz, one of the country's most celebrated wood designers.

Paper

Aromatic handmade papers made from recycled plant material – bananas, coffee,

Musical souvenirs are popular

pineapple, mango – and using natural dyes are sold as writing paper, notebooks, and bookmarks. Look for holalola, selling sophisticated and whimsical cards, stickers, calendars, and notebooks at the airport outlets or at their San José store (tel: 2234-5648; www.holalolashop.com).

Ceramics

Clay pots and vases made in the traditional pre-Columbian way in northwest Guanacaste are distinctive but very fragile. If you buy one, make sure it is well wrapped. You'll also find modern, colorfully painted and brightly glazed ceramics made by local potters.

COFFEE AND COMESTIBLES

Costa Rican coffee is among the world's best and it's relatively inexpensive. The flashiest brand is Café Britt, colorfully packaged in attractively whimsical bags. It's excellent coffee, but it's also the most expensive. If what's inside the bag matters more to you than the packaging, look for the coveted Coopedota coffee from the Tarrazú highlands.

Aside from buying directly from the coffee farms, the best place to buy coffee is at a supermarket. Auto Mercado is the classiest chain in the country and you'll find Britt coffee there, as well as much cheaper but still excellent brands, such as high-quality Café 1820. Just be sure to buy coffee marked 'puro' or 'export quality.'

As you travel around the country and notice which coffee you particularly enjoy,

don't hesitate to ask the server or restaurant owner *que marca* (which brand) they are serving. Look on supermarket shelves, too, for other local food specialties, such as Salsa Lizano, organic chocolate bars, vanilla beans, specialty herbal teas, and salty *platano* (plaintain) and yuca snacks

MUSICAL SOUVENIRS

Easy to pack, local music CDs are great souvenirs. Papaya Music specializes in Costa Rican traditional songs and upbeat dance music.

Editus, a Latin Grammy-awarded trio of guitar, violin, and percussion, combines new age and haunting melodies. One of the best souvenirs is the Symbiosis DVD, a masterpiece of music and video, celebrating the rain forest in enchanting images set to music composed and played by composer-pianist Manuel Obregón, a former minister of culture.

PANORAMIC PHOTOGRAPHY

You may have taken wonderful photos throughout your trip, but no amateur photographer can match the panoramic photos, often taken from the air, that are contained in gorgeous, high-quality coffee-table books and calendars celebrating Costa Rican landscapes, flora, and fauna. Some of the calendars also benefit conservation organizations, so your purchase is a also donation. You'll find them in souvenir shops, Librería Internacional bookstores in San José, and at the airport stores.

Teatro Nacional, San José

ENTERTAINMENT

As a capital city, San José has all the national cultural trappings – music, theater, and dance venues, along with movie theaters. But aside from a few annual music festivals, most entertainment in the hinterlands centers on nocturnal nature tours.

Costa Ricans are not night owls. After 10pm even the traffic lights in San José, the capital city, go into amber flashing mode, since there is so little traffic.

Most tourists do not come to Costa Rica for nightlife, but you can find bars and restaurants that stay open late in San José, especially in the area around the universities on the east side of San José and out in the trendy western suburbs of Escazú and Santa Ana (see page 124)

Unless you speak Spanish fluently, stand-up comedy and local theater performances are probably out, but music is universal. All across the country, you will hear Latin beats pulsing out of loudspeakers from stores, cars, bars, and restaurants.

MUSIC SCENE

The National Symphony is on stage at the Teatro Nacional from April through November, with international performers making guest appearances. Dance performances, chorale competitions, and international bands also take over the stage. Tickets are inexpensive and usually available the same day. Just experiencing the decor of the beautifully restored National Theater is worth the price of admission (www.teatronacional.go.cr).

Around the corner from the National Theater, on Avenida 2, the Art Deco-era Teatro Popular Melico Salazar (www.teatromelico.go.cr), presents musical and stage performances by local and international groups.

The San José jazz scene is pretty much limited to the intimate Jazz Café, with two branches – in downtown San Pedro and suburban Escazú (see page 124).

International Latin pop performers, such as Ricky Martin, and vintage rock bands making sentimental tours, show up in concerts at large sports stadiums in and around San José.

Credomatic Music Festival

In August, the Credomatic Music Festival (www.baccredomatic.com/es-gt/empire-music-festival) brings musicians from all over the world, and across the musical spectrum, to give concerts throughout the coun-

try in natural venues. You may have a chance to listen to a baroque quartet play a Bach fugue against the backdrop of ocean surf or the nocturnal sounds of a forest.

Envision Festival

For something entirely different and alternative, the annual, four-day Envision Festival (www.envisionfestival.com) takes place on a ranch south of Dominical, on the South Pacific coast. Billed as an event to inspire 'through art, spirituality, yoga, music, dance, sustainability, and connection to nature,' this is a New-Age, thoughtful take on 1960s 'happenings.' People of all ages – including families – come together in a makeshift village to camp, watch sunrises and sunsets, make music, watch live stage performances, and feel connected.

Traditional music

Traditional Costa Rican music is at its best played on a *marimba* (wooden xylophone). You may get a chance to hear the lively, ringing tones at a beachside barbecue or resort hotel, or catch a folkloric show in a resort hotel in Guanacaste province, noted for its folk dances.

One piece of traditional music you will hear often is the Costa Rica National Anthem. It's played every morning at 8am on radio stations. Typical of 19th-century martial tunes written for new Latin American republics, it's upbeat, inspiring, and very long. The lyrics celebrate Costa Rica's blue skies, fruitful toil, and peace.

Karaoke

Karaoke is a national craze. Amateur performers often verge on professional quality, especially in the many karaoke competitions held across the country. Feel free to join in. Beatles songs are especially popular.

CINEMA

Costa Ricans love movies. Most movie theaters are state-of-the-art, including an iMax theater in Escazú, with reclining seats and VIP lounges. Prices are half those in Europe or North America.

Many movies appear in their original version (OV) with Spanish subtitles (*subtitulado*), but many are dubbed (*doblado*), so be sure to check if you want to hear an English soundtrack. Costa Rican moviegoers love to munch on huge trays of nachos, popcorn, and snacks and they love to chat. But they will usually respond to a polite shushing.

A couple of movie theaters in downtown San José play international releases: Cine Magaly, the comfortable and roomy downtown flagship theater of a national chain; and the smaller, artsier Sala Garbo. For all movie listings in the San José area, check out: www.cinemania.co.cr.

Surfing in Nosara

ACTIVITIES

If you define sports as putting your physical fitness and skills to the test, Costa Rica offers every opportunity on land, sea, and in the air. For visitors who revel in just being outdoors and soaking up nature, less arduous activities abound.

Futbol (soccer) rules in Costa Rica. Every village has a playing field and footloose foreigners are welcome to join in pick-up games. But most visitors are here for outdoor adventures, including some adrenaline-pumping extreme sports.

WATER SPORTS

A tidal wave of water sports attracts many visitors, from surfing to whitewater rafting, snorkeling to scuba diving, kayaking to windsurfing and paddleboarding.

Since the 1960s and the release of *The Endless Summer* surfer documentary, Costa Rica has been a mecca for surfers. The best surfing, from January through April, is on the Pacific Coast, from Jacó down to Uvita, and over on the Nicoya Peninsula, from Playa Grande down to Malpaís.

From late December through March, surfers head to the Caribbean coast and the Salsa Brava waves. From April through September, the action shifts to Playa Pavones on the east side of the Golfo Dulce.

Board and equipment rentals are widely available. If you're a novice, there are plenty of surfing schools to choose from. Nosara, on the south shore of the Nicoya Peninsula, is one of the best places to learn.

Diving and snorkeling

Scuba diving and snorkeling depend on clear water with good visibility, not in great supply in Costa Rica, owing to all the muddy run off from rivers. Water tends to be clearer on the Pacific than the Caribbean coast.

The most popular diving area on the Pacific Coast is on the Nicoya Peninsula, from Playa Hermosa down to the Playas del Coco and Ocotal. Dive stores abound and prices are competitive. Expect to see large fish: giant mantas and even bull sharks. The best time of year is May through July.

Farther south, the waters around Isla del Caño, with strong currents, attract experienced divers in search of sharks. The coral reef here has the best snorkeling on the Pacific side. The island being a nature preserve, the number of boats bringing divers and snorkelers is limited – do book ahead.

On the Caribbean side, the best snorkeling is along the intermittent coral reef that runs south from Cahuita to Punta Uva. You can hire a boat to take you out from Cahuita, or swim to the close-in parts of the reef off Punta Uva beach.

Whitewater rafting

Inland, whitewater river rafting is the biggest thrill on water. The most challeng-

Exploring Tortuguero National Park by canoe

ing courses are along the Pacuare and Reventazón rivers, northeast of San José. Gentler runs, advisable for novices, are along the Sarapiquí River, north of Heredia. You can book a day trip from San José to get a taste of rafting, or set out on multi-day rafting and camping expeditions.

SPORT FISHING

Sport fishing, strictly catch-and-release, is a popular, if expensive activity, with swordfish, marlin and sailfish the main trophies. Playa Herradura and Quepos on the Pacific side have the biggest sport-fishing fleets. On the Golfo Dulce, Golfito and Playa Zancudo are the top destinations.

There are also opportunities to go out with local fishermen in small boats, in Dominical and Uvita on the south Pacific coast, to catch snapper, tuna, and roosterfish that you can take home and eat.

HIKING, CLIMBING, CYCLING

Hiking in the national parks and mountain climbing top the list of demanding sports, and cycling, despite dangerously narrow and steep roads, is becoming very popular. Many visitors, though, will probably spend much of their time walking forest trails in any one of Costa Rica's 26 national parks.

Nature walks take on a whole new dimension when accompanied by a knowledgeable, bilingual guide. Even when you see nothing beyond varying shades of green, a guide will point out flora and fauna right under your nose.

NATURE-WATCHING

Bird-watching and wildlife photography are the most popular tourist activities on land. With more than 900 bird species to spot, most serious birders manage to chalk up 200 to 300 new birds on an intensive birding tour. Beyond colorful (and noisy) toucans and scarlet macaws and fairy-like hummingbirds, the most sought-after bird is the aptly named resplendent quetzal. Your best chance of seeing one is with a birding guide, in the highland forests of Cerro de la Muerte, south of San José, and in Monteverde's cloud forest.

Photography is now so popular that guides and lodges offer special tours, complete with viewing platforms equipped with electricity to charge up camera and computer batteries. Paraíso Quetzal and Savegre Hotel, both in the highlands, are prime viewing spots.

GOING TO EXTREMES

More visitors are challenging themselves with thrilling adventure sports, whether its bungee-jumping from a bridge, rappelling down a waterfall, climbing a 30-meter (100ft) tree with ropes and pulleys and spending the night on a treetop platform, or zip-lining through the forest canopy.

Out on the water you can learn to windsurf on gusty Lake Arenal or Bahina Salinas, or parasail over the ocean. Up in the air, you can jump off a mountain and paraglide, or fly high in an ultralight.

HISTORY: KEY DATES

Since impoverished Spanish colonial days, Costa Rica's history has been a slow but steady march to a democratic, social-welfare state. With no armed forces and no guerrilla groups, the country is the most peaceful and safest country in Central America.

PRE-COLUMBIAN

4000–1000 BC	Earliest settlements in Central America based on crop cultivation.
1000 BC–AD 1500	Farming communities establish trade and communication links.

DISCOVERY AND SPANISH CONQUEST

1502	Christopher Columbus 'discovers' Costa Rica.
1572	Colonial era begins. Without mineral resources and slave labor, colony remains poor and neglected for 250 years.

LIBERATION

1823	Civil War between conservative imperialists and republicans who prevail and move capital from Cartago to San José.
1824	Guanacaste province, in Nicaragua, annexed to Costa Rica.
1825	First constitution of the free state of Costa Rica promulgated.

19TH CENTURY

1832	First coffee exports to Europe, via Chile, creating new wealth.
1838–42	Dictatorship of President Braulio Carrillo.
1848	Declaration of the Republic of Costa Rica.
1858	Costa Rica defeats William Walker, who tried to turn Central America into a colony of the southern southern states of the US.
1870	Tomás Guardia Gutiérrez seizes power; new liberal constitution.
1882	Death penalty abolished.
1886	Introduction of compulsory education.
1890	Atlantic Railroad is completed. Creation of the United Fruit Company. Costa Rica becomes the prototype Banana Republic.

Detail of a mural showing a coffee harvest

20TH CENTURY

1919	Popular uprising ends two-year dictatorship backed by coffee barons.
1931	Manuel Mora forms Communist Party.
1934	Plummeting coffee prices create hardship. Strikes against United Fruit Company leads to wage guarantees and the right to unionize.
1939	New president Dr Rafael Angel Calderón Guardia creates social-security system, a labor code, and social guarantees.
1941	Costa Rica joins Allies and confiscates German-owned lands.
1948	Calderón Guardia annuls election results. Civil War erupts. Junta led by José Figueres takes power.
1949	Under new constitution, the army is disbanded. Figueres hands over power, but governs again from 1953–8 and 1970–4. Afro-Caribbeans and women enfranchised.
1955	First national park established at Poás Volcano.

MODERN TIMES

1979	The US pours money into Costa Rica for hospitals, schools, and infrastructure. Mass influx of Nicaraguans fleeing their Civil War.
1986	Oscar Arías Sánchez elected president; he wins the Nobel Peace Prize in 1987 for his role in restoring peace to the region.
1991	A massive earthquake strikes Limón province, causing death and extensive damage, destroying the Atlantic railroad.
1998	President Miguel Angel Rodriguez encourages foreign investment and privatizes state companies.
2006	Oscar Arias re-elected to unprecedented second term as president and signs US-Central American Free Trade Agreement (CAFTA).
2009	Devastating earthquake in the Varablanca area.
2010	Laura Chinchilla elected first woman president of Costa Rica.
2014	Luis Guillermo Solis Rivera elected president. National soccer team (La Sele) reaches quarterfinals at World Cup in Brazil.
2015	At the Paris Climate Conference, Costa Rica makes a pledge to be carbon neutral by 2085, not 2021 as previously promised.
2018	The International Court of Justice rules in Costa Rica's favor in a long-running border dispute with Nicaragua. Carlos Alvarado, of the Citizens' Action Party (PAC), is elected president, promising to rein in the deficit, improve education, and maintain ecological standards.

BEST ROUTES

Chilling in Parque Morazán

SAN JOSÉ

This capital city may not win any beauty contests but downtown's Barrio Amón has architectural charm, artsy cafés and pleasant green oases. Top off a leisurely morning stroll with an afternoon gazing at gold and jade in the city's two world-class museums.

DISTANCE: less than 3km (2 miles)
TIME: a half day walking; a full day if you visit the Gold or Jade museum.
START: Parque Morazán
END: Plaza de la Cultura or the Jade Museum
POINTS TO NOTE: Early morning, especially on a Saturday, is ideal before traffic builds up. City sidewalks are not well maintained and crossing streets sometimes involves leaping over a deep gutter, so walk carefully. Many intersections do not have pedestrian signals, so pay close attention to traffic coming to a full stop before you cross. Carry as little as possible with you, just as much money as you need for the day and tuck your camera or cell phone away in a sturdy bag worn diagonally across your chest. Walking the narrow streets in San José requires close attention. Pavements are in various stages of disrepair.

Thanks to wealth generated by the late 19th-century coffee boom, San José enjoyed an architectural and cultural golden age in the early 1900s. Remnants of that era's neoclassical architecture, European elegance, and whimsical Caribbean-colonial style survive in Barrio Amón. This downtown neighborhood is also home to trendy art spaces, trendy cafés, and a trio of inviting green spaces where you can watch the passing parade of modern San Joséfino daily life.

EL PURO CENTRO (DOWNTOWN)

Start your walking tour in **Parque Morazán ❶**, an island of calm encircled by a busy traffic circle. Presiding over the park is the classical, round **Templo di Música**, the city's official symbol. You might catch a band concert in progress, but, more likely, a group of teenagers will be sitting on the temple steps, gathered around a guitar player.

Tall jacaranda trees provide shade for stone benches and grassy areas bordered by trimmed flowering hedges. This city park has the distinction of being one of the few manicured parks where you are allowed to lounge on the grass.

Barrio Amón murals   *Edificio Metálico*

Despite the general rule of no *escenas amorosas* (amorous displays) in public spaces, the park authorities have placed *El Beso* (The Kiss), a decidedly erotic statue of entwined, naked lovers, on the park's central walkway. Despite the prohibitive signs, some park-goers still find the sculpture inspiring.

At the east side of the park, cross the traffic circle – carefully, since there is no crosswalk – heading toward an alley of magnificent trees towering over a large ebony statue of **Daniel Oduber Quirós** ❷. President from 1974–78, Oduber championed reforestation and preserving natural resources. The magnificently gnarled trees are false cork trees – press a finger against the bark and you can feel the sponginess.

MONUMENTS TO PEACE

Next to the row of trees is the continuation of Parque Morazán, with a flowing fountain and a charming mosaic panel of a little girl blithely flying high on a swing, commemorating the park's alter identity as the **Parque de la Paz** ❸ (Park of the Peace). Facing the imposing metallic building across the street, to your right you'll find another memorial to peace: a statue of the bust of **Dr Carlos Luís Collado Martínez** (1918–44), a Costa Rican doctor who graduated from the University of Bologna, fought with the Italian resistance in World War II and was executed during the Nazi invasion in 1944.

EDIFICIO METÁLICO

The impressive **Edificio Metálico** ❹ (metallic building} across from the park is the **Escuela Julia Lang**, named for a 19th-century 'indefatigable educationist.'

The entirely metal building was fabricated in Belgium in 1890 and then shipped in pieces to the New World. The popular story goes that the shipment was actually destined for another country but was offloaded in Costa Rica by mistake and the Costa Ricans decided to keep it. For more than a century it was known as the Yellow Schoolhouse. It's still a school but recently it was painted a more subdued taupe with brown trim.

PARQUE DE ESPAÑA

Cross the road on the east side of the school and you enter a true city oasis of tall palms, fig trees draped with vines, and thick stands of bamboo. Opened in 1895, **Parque de España** ❺ commemorates Costa Rica's Spanish heritage. Look for the bust of Queen Isabella of Castille, statues of Juan Vasquez de Coronado (the country's founder), and an unnamed 'Conquistador.'

Hidden amid the tangle of trees and foliage is a bust of Andrew Carnegie, the Scottish-born American philanthropist, who donated funds to build the first Central American Court of Justice, based in Cartago. After an earthquake destroyed that building, the court moved to San José, into the

yellow building you'll spot across the street from the park.

CASA AMARILLA

The ornate, aptly named **Casa Amarilla** 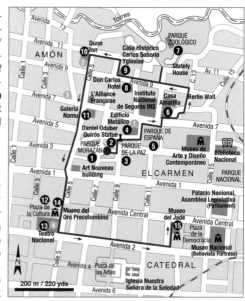⁶ facing the north side of the park was built in the 1920s. The beautifully restored building in Spanish Baroque style is now part of the Ministry of Foreign Affairs, and is used for diplomatic receptions. (The glass and concrete building next door is one of the less objectionable modern buildings in the city. It's the head office of INS, the National Insurance Institute.)

If you're ready for coffee or a full-fledged breakfast, walk 50 meters/yds east of the INS building, on the south side of Avenida 7, and enter a different kind of oasis at **La Criollita** (see ❶), part art gallery, part aviary, and all *típico* cuisine.

BERLIN WALL FOUNTAIN

Walk back along Avenida 7 and cross the busy road for a close-up look at the Casa Amarilla. Follow the curve of Calle 11A, around the fenced-in Ministry's modern yellow buildings, to Calle 13, then walk a short

block north to the corner with Avenida 9. Behind an ornamental iron fence on your left you'll see a scarred, painted section of the **Berlin Wall**, a symbol of democracy made into a fountain. Although there are elegant benches arranged around the fountain, the public is unfortunately not allowed in the enclosure.

FADED ELEGANCE

Walk west along Avenida 9 to admire the facades of the stately houses that once filled this neighborhood's streets. At the corner of Calle 11, cross over Avenida 9

Casa Amarilla

and take a very short walk north to the ornamental gates of the now defunct **Parque Zoológico Simon Bolívar** ❼. The rose-colored mansion on the west side of the street houses the **Centro de Cine**, which has free screenings of local movies. Check the schedule at www.e-park.cr.

Continue downhill on Avenida 9 past the **Don Carlos Hotel** ❽ (see page 108), occupying a charming, historic house that was once home to two country presidents. There's a peaceful inner courtyard and an excellent gift and souvenir shop. Along the hotel garden wall as you walk down the hill, stop to admire the charming painted ceramic murals, showing scenes from an idealized country life.

On the other side of the street, at the corner of Calle 7, note the green-and-white Victorian wooden mansion, with a wooden veranda. Ironically, the **Casa Histórica Carlos Saborio Yglesias** ❾, built in 1910, was recently restored by the very modern TEC University, a high-tech institution with its main campus across the street.

DUNN INN

Turn right down Calle 7 and walk north one block to Avenida 11, then turn left (west) along the avenida one block to the **Dunn Inn** ❿. This restored wooden hotel built in 1933 is notable for a street-side stained glass mural featuring tropical birds and foliage. The hotel's **Tropix Bar** is an Art Deco classic straight out of the movie *Casablanca*. Stop in for a drink.

Walk south down Calle 5, alongside the Dunn Inn and past the kitschy, open-air **Alma de Amón** (see ❷) restaurant, a good option for lunch.

CULTURE CORNER

Continue two blocks south on Calle 5. On the northeast corner of Avenida 7 and Calle 5, you'll come to a Victorian house with a wrought-iron veranda, home to **L'Alliance Française**. Stop in for coffee and croissant in the café and see what's on in the art gallery. On Friday nights, free French movies are screened.

Directly across the street you'll see the **Galería Namú** ⓫ (https://galeria namu.com; Mon–Sat 9am– 6.30pm, Sun Jan–April only 1–5pm) the country's premier collection of authentic indigenous crafts and a showcase for local artists – Borucan masks, exquisite Colombian basketry, *netsuke*-like *tagua* nut (vegetable ivory) sculptures, Guaymí embroidered dresses and dolls, and exotic one-of-a-kind wearable art. Take some time to browse through the store and chat with the friendly, knowledgeable English-speaking owners.

If it's lunch time, back track half a block along Avenida 7 to Calle 3A, and look for the blue awning at the entrance to **Delicias del Perú** (see ❸), a tiny outpost of inexpensive but flavorful Peruvian home cooking.

Inside the Museo del Oro Precolombino

PLAZA DE LA CULTURA

Head east again on Avenida 7 back to Calle 5 at the western edge of Parque Morazán, and turn right to walk south, past a block of typical souvenir shops and one of the few Art Nouveau buildings in the city, with curved ironwork gates and window details.

Three blocks on, you'll reach the edge of the **Plaza de la Cultura** ⓬, the city's lively central plaza, home to ocarina peddlers, children cavorting in a sidewalk fountain, and assorted mimes and street musicians. Presiding over the daily carnival is a stately Grande Dame, the **Teatro Nacional** ⓭, opened in 1897 and still the finest building in Costa Rica.

Modeled after the Paris Opera House, the theater's construction was financed by 19th-century, culture-hungry coffee barons who were chagrined that there was no appropriate venue in the country for the world-renowned soprano Adelina Patti. They raised the money to build the theater by levying a tax on every bag of coffee exported. Sadly, Ms Patti never did sing here.

You can take a tour of the beautifully restored theater and admire the gold, bronze, tropical woods, crystal chandeliers, velvet drapes, and marble statuary and painted ceilings. If you don't like guided tours, buy an inexpensive ticket to any night's performance and soak in the decor along with the music.

Be sure to stop in at the **Café del Teatro** (see ④), a perfect time capsule of the Belle Epoque, with marble floors and tables, spindle-wood chairs, and a painted ceiling of plump, scantily draped muses. The bonus of a café stop here, for coffee or lunch, is that your paid receipt is your ticket into the theater's elegant marble restrooms, and a chance to peek behind the red velvet curtains into the resplendent auditorium.

GOLD AND JADE MUSEUMS

From the National Theater, follow the steps down to the south edge of the plaza to find the sub terra entrance to the world-class **Museo del Oro Precolombino** ⓮ (tel: 2243-4202; https://museosdelbancocentral.org; daily 9.15am–5pm). As you descend two levels beneath the Plaza de la Cultura, you travel back in time and space to a pre-Columbian village where skilled goldsmiths fashioned the gold necklets, bracelets, breastplates, talismans, and jewelry displayed in brightly lit showcases. Along with easy-to-grasp illustrations and captions explaining the gold-making processes, there are interactive displays. You can try your skill at matching the stylized goldsmiths' versions of animals with real (taxidermy) animals.

The museum's sophisticated shop (daily 9.30am–5.30pm) is almost as interesting as the collection itself, with a treasure trove of gold-plated replica jewelry, indigenous textiles, crafts, ceramics, art books, and unique souvenirs.

Plaza de la Democracia

If you still have time and energy enough to absorb another superb collection of pre-Columbian artifacts, head east for five blocks on pedestrianized Avenida 2 to the Plaza de la Democracia and turn left (north) up Calle 13 to Avenida Central to reach the **Museo del Jade** ⑮ (tel: 2521-6610; www.museodeljadeins.com; daily 10am–5pm). Costa Rica owns the world's largest collection of New World jade, formerly housed in showcases on the top floor of an office building. The focus at this modern museum is on how the exquisite jade pieces were made and what they meant to the pre-Columbian cultures who made them. The five floors are full of color, light, and sound, and interactive exhibits, including a large sand pit where would-be archeologists can excavate hidden relics and treasures.

Food and Drink

❶ LA CRIOLLITA

Avenida 7, 50 meters/yds west of INS Building; tel: 2256-6511; Mon–Sat 6.30am–7pm, Sun 8am–7pm; $

This beloved San José institution serves excellent *comida típica* in a bright, art-filled setting. Make your way to the innermost courtyard where caged budgies happily chatter amid tropical foliage. Order a hearty *desayuno* (breakfast plate) or try the raisin-filled rice pudding with an espresso.

❷ ALMA DE AMÓN

Calle 5, 25 meters/yds north of Dunn Inn; tel: 2222-3232; Mon–Sat 6am–10pm; Sun 6am–5pm; $

The cuisine at this open-air café/restaurant covers contemporary Latin American favorites, from Cuban to Caribbean, Brazilian, and Mexican. The look is cheerfully eclectic and kitsch, centered on a huge mural of neon-colored birds wearing Carmen Miranda fruit hats.

❸ DELICIAS DEL PERÚ

Calle 3A, a few steps north of Avenida 7; tel: 2222-1959; Mon–Sat 10am–4pm (lunch only); $

A blue awning marks the entrance to this tiny Peruvian eatery. The standout dish is chicharrón de calamar, crisp calamari fritters, served with fried yucca, salad, and a dynamite hot sauce. Arrive early or late to beat the lunch-hour crowd.

❹ CAFÉ DEL TEATRO

Plaza de la Cultura; tel: 2010-1100, ext 1119; Mon–Sat 9am–4pm May–Dec; $$

Come for fruit shakes, hot chocolate, specialty coffees, and for truly fresh coffee filtered tableside. Crêpes, fancy sandwiches, and interesting salads fill out a sophisticated menu. Dessert reigns supreme, though, in this elegant Belle Epoque salon – try a slice of homemade *queque de higo*, two moist cake layers sandwiching fig conserve, and slathered with vanilla icing.

HEREDIA

Much of Costa Rica's history, early economic development, and culture revolved around coffee – growing, picking, roasting, and drinking it. To get a taste, both figuratively and literally, of Tico coffee culture, past and present, head to the hills of Heredia.

DISTANCE: Walking tour of town, 2km (1.2 miles); driving up into hills, 16km (10 miles).

TIME: A leisurely day with lunch; a packed day with afternoon coffee tour or hill drive.

START/END: San José

POINTS TO NOTE: From San José, take a taxi to Heredia, or take the train from San José's historic Atlantic Station on the south side of the Parque Centrale. The vintage train leaves as early as 4.45am; the last morning train leaves at 8am for the half-hour trip. Get there early to buy your ticket as the train fills up quickly. If you travel by train on a Saturday, be aware there is no afternoon service back to San José so pre-book a taxi or plan to stay overnight. Saturday is the best day to visit, though, as there is less traffic from San José via taxi, fewer train passengers, and it's the day of the Heredia's photogenic weekly outdoor market. As in San José, be very careful walking in town since pot-holed sidewalks can be treacherous.

Just 11km (7 miles) north of San José, Heredia was founded in 1706, long before San José. The town, poetically styled *La Ciudad de Las Flores*, City of the Flowers, harkens back to the prominent Flores family.

A bastion of coffee wealth since the late 19th century, Heredia is even more prosperous today, fueled by affluent suburbs and commercial development. But visitors can still get a feeling for Spanish colonial times with a stroll in the old town, centered on the Parque Central.

Beyond the city limits, the hills, often shrouded in mist and arched by rainbows, are still green with *cafetals* (coffee farms). Two smaller coffee towns boast impressive Gothic churches and retain a small-town way of life, based on school, church, and soccer field.

MERCADO CENTRAL

Start your walking tour of Heredia in the central covered market, the **Mercado Central ❶**, off Avenida 6

The elegant Doric columns inside the Church of the Immaculate Conception

between Calle 2 and 4. This warren of narrow passages, lined with a hodge-podge of stands, offers everything from fish, meat, poultry, cheese, fruits, and vegetables, to jewelry repair and barbershops. Despite nearby modern supermarkets and malls, many Ticos still prefer to shop the old-fashioned way, visiting vendors they have known for generations.

More than a dozen **sodas** (fast-food counters), see ❶, are scattered through the market. Choose a seat – a counter stool or a chair at a table – and order some coffee and breakfast, and sit back and watch the passing show.

Emerging into daylight onto Avenida 6, turn right (east) to the corner of Calle Central, cross the avenida and walk north two blocks aiming for the green of Parque Central. Along the narrow, busy sidewalks, you'll be treated to another mind-boggling variety of small stores and sidewalk stands bustling with customers.

PARQUE CENTRAL

Only one block square and mostly paved, the elegant **Parque Central** ❷ appears greener and larger, thanks to towering palms and fig trees shading the old-fashioned concrete benches lining the wide walkways. The center-piece of the park is the Victorian-style bandstand, where local bands still play concerts (Dec–May Thu 5pm and Sun 10pm). A cast-iron fountain, imported from England in 1879, is protected from would-be bathers by railings and is now the domain of the park's pigeons. Pick up an ice cream cone or cup at **POPS** (see ❷), on the southeast corner of the park, and relax on a park bench.

CHURCH OF THE IMMACULATE CONCEPTION

Buildings covering 250 years of history surround the park. The most impressive is the whitewashed, neo-classical **Iglesia de la Inmaculada Concepción** ❸, dating from 1797. The interior is all French elegance, with cream-colored Doric columns, topped with gold capitals and a gold *fleur de lys* frieze. Crystal chande-liers above and a diamond-patterned marble-tile floor below highlight how Costa Ricans started looking beyond Spain for inspiration. The fact that the church has withstood earthquakes is a tribute to its thick walls and low but-tresses.

CASA DE LA CULTURA

Walk down the left aisle of the church and exit into the church garden. Directly across the street (Avenida Central) is the **Casa de la Cultura** ❹, built in the colonial *bahareje* (wattle and daub) style, dating from 1792. Inside, note the floor tiles, imported

from France 200 years ago and still in excellent shape.

An art gallery near the entrance showcases local artists. The casa's main attraction is a small gem of a museum detailing the building's history through old photographs, antique furniture, and personal possessions. Originally built as a general store, the building became the residence of the influential Flores family, whose most famous son served as the country's president in 1914–17. Captions are provided in both English and Spanish, and in Braille.

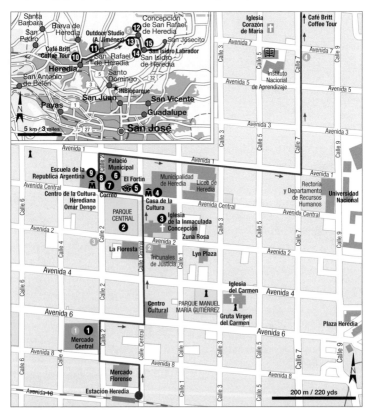

El Fortín

THE LITTLE FORT

Back on Avenida Central, head west across Calle Central to the small park with an outdoor amphitheater overlooked by a round brick tower with tiny oval windows. This odd structure is **El Fortín** ❺ (Little Fort), built in the 1870s to defend the town, which happily was never necessary. But it makes a pretty picture and now sees action as the province's official symbol.

Next door is the **Palacio Municipal** ❻, a quartet of colonial-era buildings facing a lovely courtyard and garden. The tiny complex houses municipal offices, but you can walk into the courtyard and take a peek (and a picture) of the charming garden, guarded by the Fortín.

The next building, with a grand arched entrance, is the town's impressive neo-Romanesque **Correo** ❼ (Post Office), built in 1915 and still in use. Turn the corner and you'll notice that the post office, like so many buildings of this era, has a false front, with nothing much behind the facade.

OLD TOWN VISTA

For an inkling of what early 20th-century Heredia would have looked like, turn north up **Calle 2** ❽, on the west side of the post office. This traffic-free block has handsome, restored buildings on each side and a row of tree-shaded benches down the middle.

The distinguished edifice across from the post office is the **Escuela de la República Argentina** ❾, opened in 1935 as the first teacher's college in the country. Ask politely and the guard will let you take a peek at the inner courtyard ringed by two stories of high-school classrooms.

The most remarkable aspect of this single block is the vista of green hills at both ends, reminders that Heredia is still the center of a coffee-growing district.

Christmas in Heredia

In November, it begins to look a lot like Christmas up in the hills above Heredia, where the year-round *vivero* (nursery) sells cypress trees that substitute for fir. Especially on weekends, cars along the road between San Rafael and the Braulio Carrillo Highway are topped with strapped-on trees. The most colorful sight is the array of *pastoras* (poinsettias) at the **Vivero El Zamorano**, 300 meters/yds west of the Braulio Carrillo highway. Under an acre of greenhouse roof, dazzling displays of red, white, pink, speckled, green, and new varieties are on view and for sale. For more Christmas spirit, sip a cup of hot chocolate and try an excellent pastry at the charming, riverside **Restaurante Bromelias del Río**, just 50 meters/yds west of Highway 32, which leads back to San José.

The entertaining Café Britt Coffee Tour

If you're looking for a pleasant café to sip a cappuccino or eat a light lunch, **Coffee Break** (see ③) is just across Calle Centrale, at the southwest corner of the park. For a more upscale lunch, walk north three blocks from the post office, then five blocks east through a mostly residential area to **L'Antica Roma** (see ④), Heredia's best Italian restaurant.

After lunch, if you're up for exploring the hills above Heredia, there are two options, both by taxi.

COFFEE TOUR

Less than 10 minutes away by taxi, the **Café Britt Coffee Tour** ⑩ (www.coffeetour.com; tel: 2277-1500; tours at 1.15pm and 3.15pm) offers an entertaining 1.5-hour tour, conducted by genial actor/guides who walk you through coffee fields and present a taste of traditional *campesino* life as well coffee.

HEREDIA HILLS

Another option is to hail a taxi and head for the hills to take your own coffee tour. A 10-minute drive brings you to the small coffee town of **San Rafael de Heredia** ⑪, 2km (1.2 miles) north, notable for its attractive central park and an outsize Gothic church, a landmark for miles around.

Follow the winding road 4km (2.5 miles) northeast uphill toward **Concep-**ción de San Rafael de Heredia** ⑫. You'll pass acres of glossy green coffee fields, with vistas of San José in the valley below, the Escazú mountain range to the south, and, on a clear day, the bulk of Irazú Volcano straight ahead, with fuming Volcán Turrialba to its left.

You can't miss the red and white communication tower at the crest of the hill. Next door is the **outdoor studio** ⑬ of notable sculptor **Achille Jiménez**, with monumental metal and marble sculptures on the front lawn and in the yard.

Concepción is the quintessential Costa Rican village with a soccer field bounded by a church, a vintage wooden school dating from 1890, and a small bar. Nothing much has changed in 100 years, except for a new upscale housing development across from the park and a charming café-bakery, **Prana** (see ⑤), serving *bocas* and *comida típica* with a view over the soccer field to the valley below.

SAN ISIDRO DE HEREDIA

Continue on the scenic road as it descends toward **San Isidro de Heredia** ⑭, another town founded on coffee prosperity, with wide streets and some original, one-story stucco houses. The highlight here is one of the prettiest churches in all of Costa Rica. **San Isidro Labrador** ⑮ is a Tico version of an English Gothic church, set in a garden of roses and agapanthus. High up on the white facade of the church, look for

Heredia hills

A selection of Café Britt coffees

a sculpted pair of oxen, a tribute to the ox-carts that once carried coffee to market and enriched the town. On occasion you can still spot a yoked pair of oxen trudging along the road.

From San Isidro, you can continue in the taxi back to San José (about $25) or catch Bus 436 signed 'San José X Pista' catty-corner from the southeast corner of the church.

Food and Drink

① MERCADO CENTRAL

Avenida Central; Mon–Sat 6am–6.30pm, Sun 7am–1pm; $

Whichever soda you choose, the coffee will be Tico-style, mild and milky; the food will be rice with beans and a variety of fried turnovers filled with meat, cheese, and beans. For something entirely different, try a fried sweet *platano maduro* (banana) filled with soft cheese.

② POPS

Calle Central and Avenida 2, southeast corner of Parque Central; daily 11am–11pm; $

Part of a national ice-cream chain, the flavors here change seasonally but you can usually count on mango, coconut, and rum raisin. There are a few tables to sit at, but in good weather eating in the park is more fun.

③ COFFEE BREAK

Corner of Avenida 2 and Calle 2; tel: 4001-2462; Mon–Sat 8am–7.30pm, Sun 9am–8pm; $

Café Britt coffee is served in this aptly named casual café facing the park. Along with iced coffee and every imaginable specialty coffee, there are *batidos* made with fresh tropical fruits blended with milk or water. Sandwiches and light lunches are on the menu, too. For dessert, try a sweet *empanada* filled with pineapple, guava, or *chiverre* (a kind of sweet pumpkin).

④ L'ANTICA ROMA

Avenida 7 and Calle 7; tel: 2262-9073; daily noon–11pm; $$

The first pizzeria in town with a wood-fired oven is still the best Italian restaurant and the most elegant. The menu lists 70 thin-crust pizza combinations, along with risottos, pastas, and hearty salads. The shareable *gigante* pie is half a meter (nearly 20in) wide. Treat yourself to a glass of beer or Italian red.

⑤ RESTAURANTE PANADERIA PRANA

Concepción de San Rafael de Heredia, across from soccer field; tel: 2268-3259; Mon–Fri 5.30am–9pm, Sat–Sun 7am–9pm; $

Breakfast and lunch at this hip restaurant/bakery are a bargain – *desayuno típico* for less than $5; a hearty lunch *casado* for $6 – and it's served with a village view. Colorful murals, multicolored wood furniture, an art gallery, and a quirky cactus garden add to the appeal.

La Basílica de Nuestra Señora de Los Angeles

OROSÍ VALLEY

This scenic loop winds along a wide river, through a verdant valley protected by misty green mountains. The mostly paved road takes you past coffee farms, colonial churches, thermal baths, and alfresco restaurants to a rain forest with accessible trails.

DISTANCE: 115km (71.5 miles)
TIME: one day
START/END: San José
POINTS TO NOTE: Weekdays are quieter, compared to weekends, when locals make day trips to the valley. Start out early, especially if you want to visit Tapantí. Do not attempt to visit Cartago during the first week of August, when more than a million pilgrims make an annual pilgrimage, on foot, to the basilica, clogging the roads for miles around.

Just an hour and a half's drive southwest of San José, the Orosí Valley bills itself as 'El valle más lindo de Costa Rica' – Costa Rica's loveliest valley. They have a point.

Getting here involves driving through some not-so-lovely urban and industrial areas, but the reward is a lush botanical garden devoted to orchids, spectacular views from two lookout points, a rare glimpse into Colonial times, and easy access to a world-renowned national park.

Start out early on this route, to beat the traffic and to take advantage of a morning hike in Tapantí National Park.

CARTAGO TO PARAÍSO

Heading south from San José on the Inter-American Highway, you reach the left turn into **Cartago ❶** in 25km (15.5 miles). Heading east on this wide road, turn right past the cemetery, at the sign for Paraíso. After two blocks, turn left and follow this road for 9km (5.5 miles) to Paraíso.

Just before you leave Cartago, on your left you'll see the white domes of **La Basílica de Nuestra Señora de Los Angeles ❷**, the shrine of the country's patron saint. If you want to visit the church, save it for your return journey, when it's a little easier to navigate.

LANKESTER BOTANICAL GARDEN

About 4km (2.5 miles) along the road, before reaching Paraíso, make the

On the streets of Orosí

first right turn after the Delta gas station, at the sign for **Lankester Botanical Garden** ❸ (www.jbl.ucr.ac.cr; tel: 2511-7939; daily 8.30am–4.30pm), a research facility owned by the University of Costa Rica.

There could be no greater contrast between the rather grim surrounding industrial area and this 11-hectare (27-acre) oasis. Here, paved trails wind past majestic trees laden with bromeliads to a sublime Japanese garden and to greenhouses showcasing more than 18,000 orchids belonging to over 1,000 species. Peak blooming time is February through March. Picnic areas and a botanical-themed gift shop all add to the garden's natural attractions.

MIRADOR OROSÍ

A bit of a misnomer, **Paraíso** ❹ is no paradise but a small, scruffy market town. Follow the one-way road into town (past the cemetery) and turn right when you reach the central park, at the sign for Orosí.

Follow this road downhill and soon, the lush, green landscape starts living up to the town's name. A little farther on turn right into the parking lot of the **Mirador Orosí** ❺, a beautifully landscaped lookout point with a valley view, provided free by ICT, the Costa Rican Tourism Institute.

You can climb 75 steps up to the highest viewpoint, or take the gentler paved path to the left. The spectacular view below encompasses sprawling villages nestled in the folds of the mountains, the winding river, and fertile fields.

From mid-January through the end of February, the green valley is punctuated with masses of bright-orange poró tree blossoms. The park has wide-open grassy areas, along with covered picnic tables with views, a playground, pretty flower beds and decent restrooms. (The ICT budget does not extend to toilet paper, so bring your own.)

OROSÍ

From here, the road winds steeply down. Cyclists love this downhill, so be on the lookout for individual riders and large pelotons, especially on weekends. You'll cross three narrow bridges before reaching the valley floor, where the road straightens out and widens as it approaches the town of **Orosí** ❻.

Turn right at the soccer field and park in front of the little white church of **San José de Orosí** ❼. Built in 1735, this is the country's oldest adobe church still in use.

Don't expect the kind of lavish, gilded interior common in Mexico or Ecuador, where sophisticated Jesuits built ornate churches. The interior here is rustic and intimate, more in keeping with the humble Francis-

The suspension bridge over the Río Grande de Orosí

can order that erected it. Next door, behind a pretty cloister garden, the original 18th-century Franciscan convent is now a small **Museum of Religious Art** , (Tue–Sat 1–5pm, Sun 9am–5pm) displaying some interesting household objects and relics from the convent's 17th- to early 18th-century heyday.

At the northwest corner of the soccer field, **Bar y Restaurante Coto** (see ❶) has been serving excellent *comida típica* and local coffee, with a view from its pleasant covered terrace, since 1952.

BALNEARIO AGUAS TERMALES OROSÍ

Two blocks east along the town's tidy, wide main street, turn right and drive two blocks to **Balneario Aguas Termales Orosí** ❾ (www.balneario aguastermalesorosi.com; tel: 2533-2156). This is a pleasant, well-kept complex of four pools filled with natural mineral water at a comfortable temperature of 33°C (91.4°F). You can relax and soak, or swim laps in the longest pool. A large terrace restaurant overlooks the pools.

Next door to the *balneario* is **Orosí Lodge** (see page 109), which has a pleasant terrace coffee shop (see ❷), serving a bottomless cup of local, organic coffee and cake. The store here has whimsical coffee-themed items made by local artisans.

RIVER CROSSINGS

Continue east along the main street, and turn right, a short distance past the Planta Santa María, a derelict coffee processing plant. Then make the next left to a T-junction, where local buses terminate. Take the road to the right, signed for **Parque Nacional Tapantí**, 9km (5.5 miles) southeast.

The road is paved a short distance, as far as the huge ICE electricity plant, then becomes a rougher lastre (dirt with stones) road. Go slow and enjoy the views of roadside coffee, tomato, and market greens farms that eventually give way to forest and rushing streams. You'll cross half a dozen narrow bridges until you reach the wide **Río Grande de Orosí**. The suspension bridge here is one of the few remaining bridges where you have to line up your wheels along wooden planks, one car at a time. (It's not as perilous as it sounds, but rather exciting.)

TAPANTÍ NATIONAL PARK

Turn right on the other side of the bridge and right, again, at the sign for **Tapantí National Park** ❿ (tel: 2206-5615; daily 8am–4pm). Follow the road uphill about 2km (1.2 miles) to the park entrance. You can park at the ranger station, pick up a trail map, use the restrooms, and pay the entrance fee. (Early birders can park outside the gate and enter the park before the

Cooling off in Tapantí National Park

official opening, as long as they pay the fee on their way out.)

At 1,200 meters (3,937ft) above sea level, this is prime rain forest, home to more than 400 bird species, and very popular with bird-watching groups. It's part of a huge, 590-sq-km (228-sq-mile) conservation area, but this section is easy to access, with a little more than 5km (3 miles) of varied trails. The most popular is the **Oropéndola Trail**, not far from the entrance, which leads to the river where there is a picnic area and restrooms. The river looks inviting but the current is swift, and swimming is not permitted. This is one of the wet-test national parks, so be prepared with a poncho and waterproof shoes.

Don't leave without visiting the small natural-history exhibit in the ranger station. Along with beetles and butterflies, there are alarmingly life-like taxidermy animals, including a puma poised to strike, ocelot, jaguarondi, sloth, kinkajou, and anteaters. This may be your best chance to see these park denizens up close.

If you're looking for lunch nearby, follow the sign, 2km (1.2 miles) before the park entrance, uphill to **Finca Los Maestros** (see ⑨) for fresh trout at this very rustic terrace restaurant with a panoramic rain forest view.

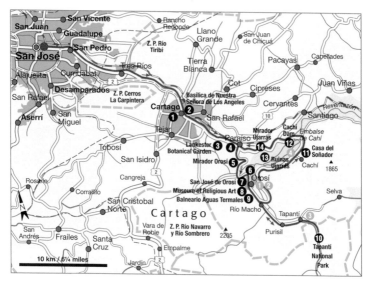

Carver at work at the Casa del Soñador

CASONA DEL CAFETAL

Retrace the road back to Orosí, where the buses park, and go straight, onto Route 224, heading east toward **Palombo**. You will soon come to another suspension bridge, over the wide Río San Carlos. Wait your turn to cross – one car at a time – and turn left, continuing on Route 224.

Past the town of Palombo, the road follows the river and the landscape once again turns to *cafetal*, tall palms and flowering hibiscus hedges. Just before the tiny community of La Alegría, you can park beside the road and walk across a **pedestrian suspension bridge** spanning the torrential San Carlos River.

The road starts to climb, passing the tidy community of Loaiza, rebuilt after a landslide. About 17km (10.5 miles) east of Orosí, turn left at the sign for Paraíso, then take the first left down a dirt road, 500 meters/yds through a huge coffee farm, to La **Casona del Cafetal** (see ④). This is the most elegant lunch stop you'll find along this route. The outdoor terrace restaurant overlooks **Lake Cachí**, the reservoir created by the nearby Cachí hydroelectric station, but at this point it is a scenic lake, framed by vine-covered arches on the restaurant's terrace. This place is popular with bus tours, so aim to arrive for an early or late lunch to secure a good table on the terrace.

Trails lead down through gardens to the lake's edge. In the trees you will see dozens of puppet oropendolas – large, noisy birds with gold-tipped tails. For a closer look, focus your binoculars or camera on their woven nests hanging from the tallest palm tree in the parking lot.

Our Lady of the Angels

If you want to visit **La Basílica de Nuestra Señora de Los Angeles** on the return trip from the Orosí Valley, continue straight north instead of taking the left turn in Cartago. Circle the church in hopes of finding parking along the streets or in the lot opposite the west front of the church.

Rebuilt following a 1926 earthquake, the multi-domed, angel-topped church has a colorful tiled floor, a wood interior faux-finished to look like marble, lovely stained-glass windows and an affecting chapel hung with amulets and notes of gratitude from supplicants whose prayers the Virgin answered.

CASA DEL SOÑADOR

Continuing on the main road, as you approach a bridge, look to the right to see the **Casa del Soñador** ⑪ (House of the Dreamer; tel: 2577-1186; daily 9am–5pm). The two-story cane structure, covered with bas-reliefs, was the

Cachí Dam   *Ujarrás ruins*

life's work of self-taught wood sculptor Macedonia Quesada. You can tour the house, admire the bas-reliefs – don't miss the Last Supper on the east side of the house – and peruse the dozens of small, whimsical wood figures carved out of coffee roots, which Quesada's sons now make and sell for $10.

CACHÍ HYDROELECTRIC DAM

One more bridge to cross and you arrive at the **Cachí Hydroelectric Dam** ⑫, one of Costa Rica's first hydroelectric projects. The dam channels water from neighboring rivers into an immense spillway and creates Lake Cachí. Built in the 1970s, the size and engineering are impressive. If such monumental structures impress you and you want a close-up look, park on the side of the road at either end of the dam, and walk along a pedestrian walkway.

UJARRÁS RUINS

Beyond the dam, the road curves and starts heading west. In 2km (1.2 miles), across from the Mini-Super del Valle, is the turnoff for the **Ruinas Ujarrás** ⑬ (daily 6am–6pm). After crossing a small bridge, turn right to reach the entrance.

The picturesque ruins of a late 17th-century stone church built by Franciscan monks are contained within a lovely, grassy park, with picnic tables and a playground. A short, paved path leads to the ruins, set among stands of giant bamboo and huge fig trees festooned with long beards of Spanish moss. The church fell into ruin during an earthquake in 1822 but the Spanish-colonial facade remains, along with remnants of the walls and main altar.

Just to the right side of the church, there's a small monument and a short path that leads to a stream flowing past what look like fields of undulating grapevines. These are actually chayote (squash) vines. Look closely through the fence and you will see the pear-shaped, hanging green squashes.

MIRADOR UJARRÁS

Back up on the main road (still Route 224), the road immediately begins a steep climb. Don't worry about stopping to catch views of the valley below, because you are almost at the **Mirador Ujarrás** ⑭ (daily 8am–4.30pm), just 2km (1.2 miles) along. Another gift from the national tourist board, this lookout is just as fabulous as the *mirador* on the other side of the valley, but not as prettily planted.

Paved paths (accessible to wheelchairs) lead to the panoramic view, seen this time from the north side of the valley. You can see the Ujarrás ruins, the lake, waves of undulat-

The pleasant Orosí Lodge Coffee Shop

ing *chayote* vines, and distant towns nestled at the base of the mountains. This lookout also has covered picnic tables with a view and restrooms.

BACK TO SAN JOSÉ

Approximately 1km (0.6 miles) past the Mirador, make a turn right for the road to Cartago, passing Lankester Gardens again. Once you reach the eastern edge of Cartago, the road veers right for one block, then left, all the way to the Inter-American Highway and back to San José.

On a clear day, as you drive north, you'll see the bulk of Irazú Volcano looming straight ahead.

Food and Drink

① BAR Y RESTAURANTE COTO

Northwest corner of soccer field, Orosí; tel: 2533-3032; daily 8am–9pm; $
You can't beat the *desayuno típico*, with *pinto*, eggs, and tortillas, for under $5 at this excellent-value terrace restaurant with a view of the colonial church. Ceviche, rice with shrimp, and grilled fish *a la plancha*. If you haven't already tried *platano con queso* – sweet plantain stuffed with melted cheese – this is your chance.

② OROSÍ LODGE COFFEE SHOP

Three blocks east of the soccer field, Orosí; tel: 2533-3578; daily 7am–7pm; $
Stop in for a bottomless cup of the lodge's light-roast, organic coffee and relax at an open-window table. Slabs of moist, homemade cake come with dollops of whipped cream. But don't bother with the disappointingly dry cookies. The owner sometimes provides musical accompaniment from a 1959 vintage jukebox.

③ FINCA LOS MAESTROS

Up steep hill, 2km (1.2 miles) before Tapantí National Park; tel: 7123-2470; B 8–10am, L 10am–5pm; $
Come to this rustic rancho for the panoramic view and for crisply fried fresh trout with French fries, *patacones* (plantain fritters), and fried yuca, washed down with beer or a fruit *naturale*, for the bargain price of $8. Colorful, naïve paintings are the work of the owner, a friendly retired school principal.

④ LA CASONA DEL CAFETAL

Off Route 224, 2km (1.2 miles) south of Cachí Dam; tel: 2577-1414; daily 11.30–4pm, lunch only; www.lacasonadelcafetal.com; $$
Elegant soups and salads with tropical and Mexican flavors make a light lunch, along with heartier fish, chicken, and pork dishes. There are also gluten-free choices. The hugely popular weekend buffet has every imaginable dish plus a notable array of coffee-flavored desserts (reservation advised for the weekend buffet).

Sunset in Cerro de la Muerte

CERRO DE LA MUERTE HIGHLANDS

No trip to Costa Rica is complete without exploring this wild and scenic highland zone south of San José. Spectacular landscapes, high-altitude coffee farms, distinct flora and fauna, and fresh mountain air promise ideal hiking, bird watching, and coffee tasting.

DISTANCE: 90km (56 miles) from San José to San Gerardo de Dota; add 18km (11 miles) if you visit Santa María de Dota.
TIME: One day if you leave very early in the morning; two days to allow time for one overnight stay.
POINTS TO NOTE: This highway route can be spectacular, especially if you start out early to avoid afternoon clouds and rain. The road has only one lane in each direction and is often traveled by large, overloaded, very slow transportation trucks. There are few passing lanes, so be prepared to drive slowly and enjoy the scenery. On Sundays, the narrow road is a favorite of hard-core cyclists, so the going can get even slower.

Named for early travelers who died from exposure while trying to cross on foot, Cerro de la Muerte, literally the 'mountain of death,' rises over 3,490 meters (11,450ft). The Inter-American Highway now winds its way up the steep slope, starting less than an hour south of San José.

Another hour's drive brings you to the junction with La Valle de Los Santos, Costa Rica's premier coffee-growing zone. A little farther on, you're in primeval oak forest, home to the country's most-sought after bird species, the resplendent quetzal.

SAN PEDRO TO CARTAGO

Start this tour early, before 7.30am, to get ahead of city traffic and fog and rain that may appear on the top of the mountain later in the day. Head south along the main road through San Pedro, on the east side of town, following signs for Cartago. Shortly after passing the big EPA hardware store, keep right to take the exit for Cartago. Keep 100 colones handy to pay a toll ahead.

This two-lane road hugs the outskirts of Cartago and divides at the main entrance to Cartago. Just past the Delta gas station, keep to the right and take the road straight ahead, signed for San Isidro de El General, passing through

an industrial zone. (If you need gas, get it at the El Guarco service station, just before the road starts up the mountain.)

CERRO DE LA MUERTE FOOTHILLS

The road climbs steeply, passing hillside farms, speckled with blue hydrangeas and white calla lilies. Fruit and vegetable stands appear along the steep road, along with signs for trout farms where you can catch your own fish and have it cooked on the spot.

About 20km (12.5 miles) on, near **Casa Mata**, you'll pass under the giant sails of the **Coopesantos Parque Eólico ❶** wind-farm turbines, brilliant white against a blue sky or ghostly giants on a cloudy day.

As the road climbs higher, you'll notice a change in the foliage along the road. Trees are now covered in moss and strung with bromeliads. Wild mountain fuchsia adds bright pink notes amid the greenery. Most notably you start to see the trademark plant of the highlands: *gunnera*, popularly known as Poor Man's Umbrella for its huge overhanging leaves.

The road quickly rises above the clouds to cool, crisp sunshine. On a clear day, you'll see fingers of clouds swirling through valleys below and over the distant Talamanca peaks.

EMPALME

At Km 51, just before the **Empalme ❷** junction, keep an eye out for an outsize orange *chorreador* (coffee apparatus) over a giant blue coffee mug, on the right side of the road. The sign reads **Mutute Café Boutique Tarrazú** (see ❶). This tiny, chic café is the showcase for award-winning coffee from the nearby Tarrazú region. Stop here for the best cappuccino or espresso you may encounter in Costa Rica, along with homemade pastries.

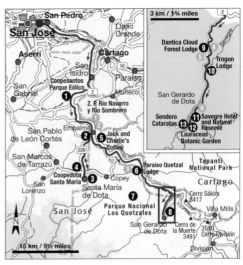

A fiery-throated hummingbird at Paraíso Quetzal Lodge

A few hundred meters/yds ahead is a bustling roadside commercial strip, with stores spilling over with cut flowers, local apples and plums, and Costa Ricans' favorite candies: marshmallows and fudge. If you're hungry, wade your way through the merchandise to the unfussy **Chespiritos 3** (see ❷), a popular cafeteria where fried trout is popular.

ROUTE OF THE SAINTS

Coffee lovers will want to make a right turn here, on the road signed **Santa María de Dota ❸**, for a short drive down into the **Ruta de Los Santos** (Route of the Saints) valley, so named because all the towns here are named after saints. This valley is the country's most scenic coffee region, with terraces of coffee bushes cut into vertiginous slopes.

About 9km (5.5 miles) down the wide, winding paved road, you'll find the **Coopedota Santa María ❹** (www.coopedota.com; tel: 2541-2828), famous not only for its coffee but also for being the first carbon-neutral coffee producer in the world. Taste the coffee for yourself at the cooperative's pleasant café. Better still, book ahead for the two-hour **Coffee Experience Tour** that takes you from bean to bag, with insights into the co-op's sustainability policies.

TOP OF THE MOUNTAIN

Back up on the Inter-American Highway, continue driving south. A series of hand-painted signs lets you know you are approaching **Jack and Charlie's Coffee ❺** (tel: 2571-1982; daily 7am–5pm). This collection of wooden shacks is worth a stop to see one-of-a-kind, handmade souvenirs, along with Boruca carved masks and colorful paintings on canvas by amiable co-owner Ana. On a clear day, you can sip a cup of excellent coffee, served with a panoramic view of two volcanoes – quiet Irazú and currently active Turrialba.

Next door at **Antigüedades Don Edwin** you might enjoy a short browse through a very eccentric and eclectic collection of 'junque,' including broken ox carts, old machinery, clocks, statues, door knockers, and vintage model cars.

PARAÍSO QUETZAL

At Km 70, look for the entrance to **Paraíso Quetzal Lodge ❻** (www.paraiso quetzal.com; tel: 2200-0241), a mecca for birders, renowned for its hummingbird gallery and resplendent quetzal sightings. Stop in for an espresso or cappucino, breakfast or lunch, and drink in the panoramic, mountain view from the restaurant's picture windows (see ❸). Then step out onto the wooden deck, where fearless hummingbirds dart, hover, and drink from hanging feeders. Be sure to have your camera in hand. If you're not staying overnight at the lodge, you can still hike the trails for a fee of $5 per person. Call ahead to reserve lunch, in case the lodge is full.

Río Savegre

LOS QUETZALES NATIONAL PARK

At Km 76, you can't miss the trucks and buses parked outside **Chespiritos 1** (daily 4am–10pm), the original truck stop with an astonishing array of edibles, including cheese-stuffed *platanos*, huge pancakes, and omelettes bursting with green beans.

Almost across the highway is the office of **Los Quetzales National Park** ❼. Trails are still being groomed at this park opened in 2005, but if you want to stretch your legs, you can check in at the ranger's office, pick up a map, and set off on a short hike. There are basic restrooms beside the office.

SAN GERARDO DE DOTA

Just 4km (2.5 miles) along, at Km 80, look for the turnoff on the right for the road to **San Gerardo de Dota** ❽. Four-wheel drive is not absolutely necessary on this steep dirt road since it's now paved on some of the trickiest curves. But low gear will come in handy on the steepest turns. It's a thrilling drive in every sense as you descend into a thickly forested valley, cut through by the turbulent Savegre River.

About 4km (2.5 miles) down the road, stop in at **Miriam's Quetzals**, aka **Comidas Típicas Miriam** (see ❹), a slightly ramshackle soda with a wood stove and, most importantly, a deck looking out onto a forest of oaks mixed with *aguacatillo* trees – the wild avoca-

does that quetzals feed on. Order some coffee or a lunchtime *casado* and step out onto the deck with your binoculars for some fantastic bird watching.

Another kilometer down the road, **Dantica Cloud Forest Lodge** ❾ (see page 109) is the most stylish lodge in the valley, with a sophisticated gallery shop (daily 10am–8pm) stocked with elegant artisanal jewelry and arts and crafts from Costa Rica and Colombia. **Le Tapir** (see ❺), the modern, glassed-in restaurant has an innovative menu, along with panoramic vistas and close-up views of resident birds visiting feeders.

Continue down into the valley, almost level with the river, and turn left at the sign for **Trogón Lodge** ❿ (see page 109). Park at the entrance and follow the stone path into an enchanted garden of fuchsias, roses, hydrangeas, and hummingbirds, centered on an ornamental pond and bordered by the Savegre River rushing over rocks. The reception area has a small gift shop with some unique jewelry and glass ornaments, worth a look and a good excuse to visit and stroll around the garden. You can also stay for a buffet lunch or dinner.

The road flattens out a bit as it follows the river. In about 2km (1.2 miles), you'll come to **Kahawa** (see ❻) (tel: 2740-1081), a modern, blonde-wood-and-stone, open-air restaurant, perched above the rock-strewn river. The focus here is on fresh rainbow trout, served with an innovative, contemporary twist.

Savegre Hotel and Natural Reserve

There's also an elegant indoor café and a store with unusual arts and crafts by a local artist.

SAVEGRE HOTEL AND NATURAL RESERVE

Just beyond Kahawa is the bridge over the river to **Savegre Hotel and Natural Reserve** ⑪ (see page 109), the first and foremost nature lodge in the valley and a magnet for birders and hikers attracted by resident naturalist guides, miles of trails, hummingbird-friendly gardens, and the sheer variety of bird life.

Day trippers can hike or bird the trails for $10 per person, or spend three hours ($20) in the **Batsu Garden**, a hide specially designed for photographers and birders, high on a hill overlooking the lodge and a fruit orchard. After a day of hiking, a visit to the lodge's **Del Río Spa** might be a good idea for a pampering or therapeutic massage (www.delriospa.com).

BOTANIC GARDEN

A few hundred meters/yds past the entrance to Savegre, you'll find a humble monument, a large stone with crossed shovels, dedicated to the 'pioneers' who first settled and tamed the valley in 1954, including the Chacón family, founders of the Savegre Hotel.

Directly across the road is the entrance to **Lauraceas Botanic Garden** ⑫ (info@lauraceas.com; tel: 8397-6071; daily 9am–4pm), a charming garden of flowering exotic plants around a pond, complete with a Japanese bridge. Trails head uphill through forest to a viewpoint with picnic tables. You can stay all day or come and go, but be sure to call ahead.

WATERFALL TRAIL

If you're up for a thrilling hike, about 200 meters/yds on the left side of the road past the monument you'll come to a chain-link gate, blocking off a dirt side road. Slip through the person-sized space beside the gate and look for the **Sendero Cataratas** ⑬ sign pointing to a trail along the river. This trail leads to two spectacular *cataratas* (waterfalls) where the Savegre River drops 50m (164ft).

The trail, about 2km (1.2 miles) long, is thrilling in itself, winding up and down but always within sight or sound of the river. You'll pass a large commercial trout farm and cross a bridge to the other side of the river, and pass by awesome, massive boulders covered in greenery, and walk thick forest alive with chattering birds. Waterproof hiking shoes or rubber boots are advised.

A note of warning: no matter how tempting, do not wade or swim in the river or near the waterfall. The current is deadly and even strong swimmers have drowned here.

Delicate presentation at Le Tapir

Food and Drink

① MUTUTE CAFÉ BOUTIQUE TARRAZU
Km 51 Inter-American Highway; tel: 2571-2323; daily 8am–6.30pm; $

'Life is too short to drink cheap coffee' is this café's motto and the owners live up to it with high-altitude coffee, freshly roasted, and expertly prepared. Choose from homemade savory empanadas and cheese tortillas or a sweet slice of fig layer cake to accompany your lovely coffee.

② CHESPIRITOS CAFETERIAS
Inter-American Highway at junction with road to Santa María de Dota, and Km 76 on Inter-American Highway; daily 4am–10pm; $

This chain of roadside cafeterias is the best and cheapest introduction to home-style Tico food. Think soups, omelets, empanadas, fried chicken, and rice and beans. For less than $5, you can sit down to a plate of whole fried trout or a breaded trout filet with vegetable trimmings.

③ PARAÍSO QUETZAL LODGE
Km 70 on Inter-American Highway; www.paraisoquetzal.com; tel: 2200-0241; daily 7am–8pm; $

Whether or not you are a bird watcher, don't miss this chance to sip excellent coffee or eat a typical breakfast served with a panoramic valley view and an ongoing spectacle of hummingbirds zipping to and from feeders on the deck.

④ COMIDAS TÍPICAS MIRIAM
San Gerardo de Dota road, 4km (2.5 miles) from Inter-American Highway; tel: 2740-1049; daily 7am–7.30pm; $

Morning coffee, a *típico* breakfast, or lunch come with the chance to bird-watch from the wooden deck overlooking the garden (early mornings or late afternoons are best). At dinner, pastas and whole fried trout are on the menu.

⑤ LE TAPIR
Dantica Cloud Forest Lodge, San Gerardo de Dota road, 5km (3 miles) from Inter-American Highway; tel: 2740-1067; www.dantica.com; daily 7am–8.30pm; $$$

Come for breakfast or à la carte lunch/dinner in this stylish, glass-walled restaurant. The sophisticated menu has a European slant with the use of fresh herbs, brandy, and wine. Lunch is casual, with crêpes, soups, and sandwiches on freshly baked bread. At dinner, fairy lights and wine (imported) make for romantic dining. Reservations are a must for dinner.

⑥ KAHAWA
San Gerardo de Dota Road, 8km (5 miles) from Inter-American Highway; tel: 2740-1081; daily 7.30am–6pm; $$

Fresh trout rules supreme here, served in myriad ways: smoked, in a bun, ceviche-style, in a taco, in a coconut sauce, or standout *chicharrón*-style – lightly battered and fried and served with tangy tartare sauce and plentiful fries. Beer, fruit *naturales*, and excellent coffee wash it down. No dinner except by reservation for six or more diners.

Mt Chirripó in all its glory

ALONG THE SPINE OF COSTA RICA

This scenic drive follows the Inter–American Highway from its highest point along the country's spine, passing through varying habitats – from highlands to middle elevations to lowlands – opening up panoramic views along the way.

DISTANCE: 67km (41.5 miles)
TIME: A leisurely day with stops or two days if you overnight and go on an early-morning hike.
START: Km70 on Inter-American Highway
END: San Gerardo de Rivas
POINTS TO NOTE: The best time to drive this route is on a weekend, especially a Saturday when all the food stores and restaurants are open along the road to San Gerardo de Rivas. The road is well paved as far as San Gerardo de Rivas, but it narrows considerably and then becomes a precipitous dirt road that requires a 4X4 vehicle. If you are planning to hike in Cloudbridge, it's a good idea to park your car and include the walk up to the Cloudbridge trails as part of your hike.

This route picks up where Route 4 ends, at Km 80 high up on the Inter-American Highway, and heads south to the town of San Isidro de El General, also known as Pérez Zeledón.

The route then veers east on a side road, climbing up toward Mt Chirripó, the country's highest peak. The hike to the summit requires extreme fitness and planning ahead. If you're not up to a strenuous hike, the road to the trailhead is an adventure in itself, both gastronomically and scenically.

CERRO DE LA MUERTE TO PERÉZ ZELEDÓN

From Km 80, this two-lane section of the Inter-American Highway keeps climbing, cutting through highland habitat, characterized by huge, umbrella-like *gunnera* plants, pink *milflore* bushes, and tall mountain nettle with purple flowers. Most days, you will find yourself above the clouds.

About 10km (6 miles) on, the habitat segues into *páramo*, a wind-blown, treeless, sub-Alpine region with grasses and gnarled shrubs. You've reached the top of the road – at an altitude of around 3,350 meters (10,990ft) when you spot a ridge lined with communications towers.

Farmers' market in San Isidro de El General

ON THE WAY DOWN

At Km 95, stop in at **Restaurante La Georgina** (see 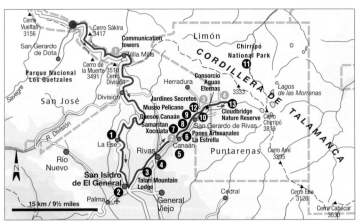), notable for providing hot chocolate and carrot muffins since 1947. You can warm up while watching hummingbirds buzz around the hanging feeders.

The road winds quickly down, sometimes passing through clouds again, and when you emerge from the clouds, you'll see the peaks of the Talamanca Mountain to your left. The most pronounced curve in the road is near Km 123, approaching the scattered community of **La Ese** ❶ (literally 'the S'). Keep an eye out for roadside kiosks displaying handcrafted, smooth, wooden bateas (serving platters), curved baguette bread holders, spoons, and bowls made by local artisans.

South of La Ese, the landscape changes to middle-elevation *cecropia* trees and ferns. Just past a faux castle on your right, the first view of the Valle de El General opens up.

SAN ISIDRO DE EL GENERAL

The general in the town's name refers to the Río El General that runs through this fertile valley. **San Isidro de El General** ❷ is the largest town in the southern zone and it is beyond bustling. A 1950s-era cathedral with two tall towers overlooks a pleasant central park. But unless you need to shop or visit an ATM, a hospital, or a gas station, it's better not to get mired in the confusing town traffic.

Stay on the Inter-American Highway, past all the gas stations, fast-food chains, and auto-supply stores, driving

Alpine moor (páramo) landscape inside Chirripó National Park

over a multi-lane bridge. Get into the left lane, and at the first traffic light, where there's a sign for Parque Nacional Chirripó, take the left turn, angling up a steep drive. Turn left at the top onto Route 242. After passing the southern branch of UNA, the national university, the road starts to climb and green mountains rise up straight ahead.

CLIMBING THE MOUNTAIN

Five kilometers (3 miles) on, **Talari Mountain Lodge ❸** (see page 113) has 8 hectares (20 acres) of forest with 2km (1.2 miles) of groomed trails through bird-filled woods and along the Río Buenavista. A day pass to roam the trails is $10, or you can come for a light, elegant lunch in the terrace restaurant and watch the action at the busy bird-feeders.

Continue on Route 242 to **Rivas ❹**, past the school and church. At the end of the wide main street, the paved road becomes a dirt road. Make a right turn here, up the paved road signed for Chirripó. The road climbs past the tidy small community of **Guadalupe de Ríos**. At **Chimirol**, you'll catch views of the Río Chirripó running headlong over huge boulders. Across the bridge over the Río San Josécito, you enter the village of **Canáan ❺**, which proudly announces its fresh altitude of 1200 meters (about 4,000ft).

This is the area's gastronomic hub. (If you're keen on sampling all the local food, be sure to make this drive on a Saturday,

when everything is open.) First stop is aromatic **Panes Artesenales La Estrella ❻**, across from the soccer field, for warm baguettes, ciabatta, and round loaves of sourdough, plain or spicy. Iced cakes and sweet dessert breads go well with an espresso made with local Ventisqueros coffee, served on the bakery's porch.

Next door is **Batsú Gastropub** (see ❷), a hip bar-restaurant with a sunlit terrace and wide-ranging menu. It's a good place to meet locals and other visitors, especially when there's live music some Saturday nights.

Chocolate and cheese

Less than 100 meters/yds up the road, **Samaritan Xocolata ❼** (Mon–Sat 10am–4pm) is an organic chocolate factory offering an array of freshly made truffles with exotic flavors, chocolate bars, and homemade ice creams. Do also try the frozen banana on a stick, encased in thick, dark chocolate. Take a seat on the veranda Chocolate Lounge and enjoy a cup of thick, hot chocolate.

A stone's throw away is **Quesos Canáan ❽**, an artisanal cheese factory, specializing in mature Swiss-style cheese using local milk from the Mata family's farm. The factory came about when a Swiss traveler spent time in the area and taught the Mata family how to make Swiss cheese. Take a short tour to learn how the cheeses – plain, herbed, or spicy – are made in a sustainable way, or just buy some for a picnic with fresh bread from the bakery.

Mountain lodging

Continue uphill a short way and on the right is the entrance to **Río Chirripó Retreat** (see page 113), a luxurious, yoga-centered riverside lodge set in a garden paradise. The Chirripó River provides a soothing soundtrack of rushing water and the views here are reminiscent of Nepal.

Less than 100 meters/yds up the road, on the left, is the steep driveway up to **Hotel de Montaña El Pelicano** (see page 113), not only a great budget hotel for hikers and birders, with panoramic views, but also home to the delightful and unique **Museo Pelicano** ❾. Housed in a rustic cabin, wrapped round by a huge serpent made from a thick vine, the museum showcases decades of folk-art, wood and stone sculptures created by Don Rafael 'Macho' Elizondo, a self-taught sculptor who has an uncanny eye for seeing birds and animals in broken tree branches and river stones. His signature piece is a large pelican made from a river-tossed tree trunk – hence the name of the land-locked lodge.

SAN GERARDO DE RIVAS

Just past the next bridge is **El Descanso** (see ❸), a small family-run hotel and restaurant with a standout young chef who transforms fresh local ingredients into sophisticated cosmopolitan dishes.

In the center of **San Gerardo de Rivas** ❿, at the south end of the soccer field, you'll find the office of the **Consorcio Aguas Etternas** (www.chirripo.org), the local cooperative in charge of all the logistics for a hike through **Chirripó National Park** ⓫; at 3,820 meters (12,533ft) this is Costa Rica's Everest. Hikers generally spend three days here – one day climbing up, a second day summiting peaks and a third day descending. Overnights are in a Spartan mountain hostel. Hostel space and hikers on the environmentally sensitive trails are strictly limited so you must reserve well in advance.

Secret gardens and trout ponds

Past the church at the north end of the soccer field, the paved road becomes a narrow, dirt road. In 250 meters/yds, where the road forks, take the left fork a few meters/yds to the **Jardines Secretos** (Secret Gardens) ⓬, an enchanting garden filled with orchids, bromeliads, heliconias, and eight lily ponds fed by a mountain stream that tumbles over huge boulders. For a small fee you can walk a 1km (0.6-mile) path up to a viewpoint with a spectacular view of the Talamancas. The adjoining open-air restaurant serves breakfast, with homemade bread, starting at 7am, a perfect time for bird-watching.

Up the same dirt road, 100 meters/yds farther on, an entirely different scene awaits. At rustic trout farm **Truchero Los Cocolisos** (see ❹), you fish for your trout lunch in a fountain-fed pond set in the jungle. The fun lies in where you choose to eat – either in the castaway-island tree house perched above the pond, or at a private covered picnic table beside a fast-moving stream where you can also take a dip.

San Gerardo de Rivas, a good base from which to explore Chirripó National Park

CLOUDBRIDGE

Returning to the fork, this time take the dirt road to the right. This is a very narrow, winding road so drive with extreme caution. In just a few hundred meters/yds you'll pass the **MINAE National Park Office**, where hikers with reservations to climb Chirripó sign in the day before they set off around 4am the next morning to make the climb.

If a 16km (10-mile) hike in high altitude is not your thing, continue on this dirt road 2.5km (1.5 miles) to the **Cloudbridge Private Nature Reserve ⓭**, with 12km (7.5 miles) of trails, including an easy one to a waterfall and 4km (2.5 miles) of trail within the Chirripó National Park. Admission is by donation. This road is very rocky and narrow and requires a 4X4. It's a good idea to park your car and include the walk up to the Cloudbridge trails as part of your hike.

Food and Drink

❶ RESTAURANTE LA GEORGINA
Km 95 on the Inter-American Highway; tel: 2200-4313; daily 7am–6pm; $
Along with a buffet of hot food, there are fresh-baked muffins and hot chocolate. Perch on a stool at the back counter and you'll be nose to bill with hovering hummingbirds.

❷ BATSÚ GASTROPUB
Main Street, Canáan; tel: 8879-6538; Mon, Wed–Sun 11am–9pm, Tue 3–9pm; $$
Come for bar food – think Buffalo wings or bruschetta topped with local goat cheese – or for mains, from sesame-flavored tuna steaks to filet mignon in a red-wine mushroom sauce. The sunny terrace is a draw, as is the youthful vibe and casual setting.

❸ RESTAURANTE EL DESCANSO
Entrance to San Gerardo de Rivas; tel: 2742-5061; daily 7am–7.30pm, Sun breakfast only; $$

Chef Esteban Acuña brings his cosmopolitan culinary skills, learned in California, to the sophisticated menu at this small gourmet restaurant. The adjoining herb garden provides the flavouring for local trout, stuffed with mushrooms and ham. An array of soups – carrot, squash, sopa negra – and a tofu green curry will make vegetarians happy. Divine desserts include a chocolate volcano cake and a coconut-caramel flan.

❹ TRUCHERO LOS COCOLISOS
250 meters/yds east of MINAE office, then north 100 meters/yds, San Gerardo de Rivas; tel: 2742-5023; Sat–Sun 10am–5pm, call ahead for weekdays; $ (no credit cards)
This is a delightful alfresco eating experience. Fish for your own meal or let the owners catch a trout for you. Enjoy the sound of the rushing river and birds calling and views of the surrounding jungle flora while your trout is fried *entero* (whole) or *a la plancha* (fileted and grilled) and served with rice, French fries, pico de gallo (fresh salsa), and fresh fruit juice.

Fiery–billed aracari

VALLE DE EL GENERAL

This route starts at San Isidro de El General and travels southeast across the wide Valle de El General, past vast plains of pineapple and sugar cane farms, with the Talamanca Mountains providing a stunning backdrop.

DISTANCE: 136km (84.5 miles) without detours

TIME: Full Day

START: San Isidro de El General

END: San Vito

POINTS TO NOTE: Large, slow transportation trucks can be difficult to pass since most of Route 2 is one lane in each direction, so take care when passing. Route 237 is paved and in good condition, but watch out for developing potholes. Driving to the Boruca village in Terraba requires a 4X4, especially if the weather has been wet. Instead of returning to San Isidro by the same route, take the steep, scenic drive south from San Vito to Ciudad Neilly, then head north on the Inter-American Highway, meeting up with the Costanera Highway (Route 34) in Palmar Norte. Continue up the Pacific Coast to Dominical and then go east on Route 243 back to San Isidro de El General. Or continue on Route 34 all the way up the coast to Orotina, and take the toll road, Route 27, east to San José.

The drive then follows the Río El General past indigenous communities, before climbing to a high ridge between two valleys. The final destination is San Vito, settled by Italian immigrants in the 1950s and now home to the country's most famous botanical garden and the top birding hotspot in the country.

LOS CUSINGOS BIRD SANCTUARY

Driving south on the Inter-American Highway, the first interesting detour is to **Los Cusingos Bird Sanctuary ❶** (www.cct.or.cr; tel: 2738-2070; Mon–Sat 7am–4pm, Sun 7am–1pm). About 6km (3.7 miles) south on Route 2 watch for the Ferretería Palmares and make a left turn to the small town of Peñas Blancas and follow signs another 7.8km (4.8 miles) to the sanctuary.

This was the rustic home, for six decades, of Alexander Skutch, the pioneering, neo-tropical ornithologist who put Costa Rica on the bird-watching map. The 78-hectare (190-acre) forested preserve is a pilgrimage for

Pineapple plantation　　　　　*A luxury villa suite at Hacienda Alta Gracia*

bird-watchers and still home to 200 species of birds, including fiery-billed araçaris (*cusingos* in Spanish), for which the preserve is named. For a guided tour call ahead, or just drop in and hike the 2km (1.2-mile) trail (charge for both).

HACIENDA ALTA GRACIA

Back on the Inter-American Highway, another 13km (8 miles) south, watch for the left turn on Route 326 for Cajón and a sign beside the roadside Hawaii restaurant pointing to **Hacienda Alta Gracia** (see page 113) an ultra-luxurious hilltop collection of private villas with a stable of horses to ride, a hilltop spa and pool, and top-notch restaurants.

For the next 40km (25 miles), the road passes flat tracts of pineapple plantations, a huge Del Monte juice-processing plant and huge

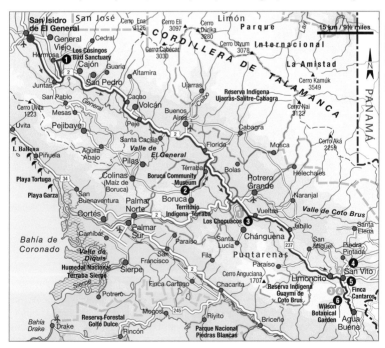

Talamanca Mountains in the mist

expanses of sugar cane. Off in the distance, to your left (east) the jagged profile of the Talamanca Mountains provides a scenic backdrop.

You'll overtake (with care) wide, ribbed wagons carting harvested cane to rather unsightly processing plants, belching smoke when operational. Huge transportation trucks lumber along bearing tons of pineapple. It's an eyebrow-raising insight into how cane becomes sugar and how pineapples, grown in a monoculture sustainable only with the heavy use of chemicals, are produced.

At the exit for Buenos Aires, there's a good roadside stop, La Flor de Sabana (tel: 2730-0256; 6am–10.30pm), with a convenience store, a food buffet, and decent restrooms. Across the highway is a produce stand with local fruits, including pineapples.

TERRABA

Another 11km (7 miles) south on the highway, watch for the turnoff to **Terraba** and the sign for **Territorio Indigena Terraba**. This rough road – 4X4 advised – leads to the main settlement of the Borucas. This is a rare opportunity to learn about the culture of one of the country's eight surviving indigenous groups in the **Boruca Community Museum** ❷ (www. boruca.org; to arrange a tour, call José, 8771-1138, or, for information in English, call 8381-4369) followed

by a walk through the village to craft workshops where traditional wooden masks are carved and painted, and cotton textiles are woven and sewn into attractive and useful souvenirs.

PASO REAL

In 20km (12.5 miles) you reach the Paso Real Bridge over the wide Río Terraba. Once across the suspension bridge, make a sharp left onto Route 237, signed for San Vito. The paved road begins to climb up to a high ridge, with panoramic views south, into the Valle de Coto Brus and north, over a wide plain with the vast Talamanca range rising in the distance. On a clear day, this drive is breathtaking.

About 8km (5 miles) along, **Los Chocuacos** ❸ (tel: 6080-6742) is an idyllic bird sanctuary, centered on a pond, where boat-billed herons – *chocuacos* – build their nests in trees along the shore. Other birds abound in the lush preserve, which also has a **restaurant** (see ❶) serving an excellent traditional tilapia lunch under a high, cone-shaped, wooden *palenque* roof.

SAN VITO

In about 30km (18.5 miles) you reach **San Vito** ❹, at a refreshingly cool altitude of 960 meters (3,150ft). The area was settled in the early 1950s by northern Italian immigrants, encouraged by incentives from the Costa

Wilson Botanical Garden   *View from Casa Botania*

Rican government. It's now the commercial hub of the **Coto Brus** coffee region. Nearby large indigenous preserves are home to Guaymí, who work mostly in the surrounding coffee *fincas*. You can recognize the Guaymí women by their colorful, intricately embroidered cotton dresses.

Some Italian features remain, such as the statue to the Italian pioneers in front of the Dante Alighieri Society; **Pizzeria Liliana** (see ❷), still the best Italian restaurant in town; and the pink-and-purple-painted Panadería & Pastelería Flor, half-way down the steep main street, serving excellent coffee and pastries at a sidewalk café.

FINCA CANTAROS

The road dips down through town, past the hospital and cemetery, and continues south past rolling hillsides, reminiscent of Tuscany, except for the tall palm trees in place of cypress trees.

Finca Cantaros ❺ (https://finca cantaros.com; tel: 2773-3760), 3km (2 miles) south of town, is a captivating crafts gallery in a restored farmhouse, stocked with carefully selected handicrafts and art by local indigenous artisans and artists.

Behind the shop is a 7-hectare (17-acre) private preserve, laced with trails that lead to a lake and a pre-Columbian cemetery with a 1,600-year-old petroglyph. At the preserve's

highest point, there are spectacular views to the east as far as Panama. Picnic tables are scattered throughout, and campers can pitch their tent for $10.

CASA BOTANIA

Around 1km (0.6 miles) down (south) the road is **Casa Botania B&B** (see page 113) owned by a Belgian-Costa Rican couple who provide the best of both continents – gourmet European breakfasts and expert naturalist tours. The terrace **restaurant** (see ❸) sometimes offers gourmet vegetarian dinners, by reservation, to non-guests.

WILSON BOTANICAL GARDEN

The ultimate experience in tropical botany awaits at the **Wilson Botanical Garden** ❻ (https://tropicalstu dies.org/lascruces), part of the Las Cruces Biological Station run by the university-affiliated Organization for Tropical Studies (OTS). Trails wind through the extensive collections of artistically arranged heliconias, bromeliads, tree ferns, orchids, palms, and begonias.

Birds abound – the garden and environs is the hottest birding spot in the country, with more than half of the country's total number of species recorded. Along with garden tours led by biologists and botanists, there are

Hanging in there

free birding tours on the second and fourth Sunday of each month, starting at 7.30am, led by members of the San Vito Birding Club (https://sanvitobird club.org) who can provide binoculars and field guides.

Guests in the garden's comfortable bungalows join researchers and students at family-style meals and are invited to hike the Río Java trail in the garden's forest preserve, home to more birds and wildlife, including plenty of monkeys.

Another excellent lodging option, across the road from the entrance to Wilson, is **Cascata del Bosco Hotel, Restaurant & Bar** (see page 113). Along with spacious round cabins and a lively, open-air restaurant (see ❹) specializing in BBQ, the grounds here include giant stands of bamboo and forest trails for walkers and birders.

Food and Drink

❶ LOS CHOCUACOS

Inter-American Highway, 8km (5 miles) south of Real Paso bridge; tel: 6080-6742; $

Come for the birds and stay for lunch in a large, open-air *palenque* (traditional hut) with a soaring conical roof. The good-value set lunch is filet of tilapia, rice and beans, salad and *piccadillo* (diced vegetables), *patacones* (plantain fritters), and dessert.

❷ PIZZERIA LILIANA

Uphill, west of central plaza, San Vito; tel: 2773-3080; daily 10am–10.30pm; $

Authentic pizza and homemade pastas rule at this traditional Italian restaurant, with a plant-filled covered terrace. The pasta specialty is *macaroni sanviteña*, with ham and mushroom in a white sauce. It's one of the few restaurants in town that's open late.

❸ CASA BOTANIA

5km (3 miles) south of San Vito on Route 237; tel: 2773-4217; www.casabotania.com; $$

The Belgian cook here has applied continental techniques to local tropical ingredients to create sophisticated, savory vegetarian fare, accompanied by lovely French wine. Desserts are divine and the setting is a draw, with a terrace overlooking the mountain. B&B guests only, no walk-ins.

❹ CASCATA DEL BOSCO RESTAURANT/ BAR

200 meters/yds south of Wilson Botanical Garden, on Route 237; tel: 2773-3208; www.cascatadelbosco.com; Tue–Sun 11am–9pm; $

Breakfast, lunch, or dinner, the food at this alfresco, casual restaurant tends toward American-style BBQ ribs, steaks, and chicken, with tropical accents. No surprise, since the owner is an ex-pat American. Homemade muffins and desserts are welcome treats. You're likely to meet English-speaking expats at the popular bar here.

Playa Ventanas

SOUTH PACIFIC COAST

With miles of undeveloped beaches, stunning Pacific sunsets, and a sophisticated restaurant scene balanced by a casual surfer vibe, this coastline drive is unmatched for natural beauty and easy access to adventures on land and sea.

DISTANCE: 108km (67 miles)
TIME: Two to three days with stops
START: San Isidro de El General
END: Sierpe
POINTS TO NOTE: Although the distances are short, you'll need time to sample beaches, tours and restaurants along this route and spend at least one night to be sure of seeing at least one sunset. On the Costanera Highway you will see some kilometer-marker signs to help you navigate along the road. This wide, smooth route is also used by transportation trucks driving between Mexico and the Panama Canal, so exit and join the highway carefully.

Sun-drenched beaches abound in Costa Rica but nowhere else can you find beaches backed by a long ridge of high hills blanketed in forest coming right down to sea level.

Visitors are spoiled for beach choices, from Dominical's popular surfing stretch with a lively bar scene, south to Playa Ventanas where you may have the beach all to yourself.

Still free from package-tour crowds and large concrete hotels, this coastal region instead features small-hotel options. Safari-tent eco-lodges to ultra-luxe boutique hotels are all tucked into the hilltop greenery above the smoothly paved, wide Costanera Highway.

SAN ISIDRO TO THE PACIFIC OCEAN

The most dramatic and scenic drive to the coast is along paved Route 243, which quickly winds its way up from San Isidro in the Valle de El General to cross the coastal mountain range and then descend to sea level. The distance to the coast is only 35km (22 miles), but count on an hour's drive, given all the road's twists and turns and the possibility of mist in the mountains.

As the road climbs, you'll pass open-air mirador restaurants taking advantage of the valley views. At the top, you'll drive through Tinamaste and Platanillo, two small towns hugging the highway,

each with a church and school, and a few stores and *sodas*.

DESCENT TO DOMINICAL

As the highway winds downhill, watch for the sign for **Parque Reptilandia** ❶ on the right (crreptiles.com; daily 9.30am–4.30pm), with 70 terrariums housing more than 80 species of snakes, frogs, turtles, and lizards, including a Komodo dragon. Naturalist-led tours are a hit with kids. If you're not squeamish, the snakes are fed lunch, fresh and alive, on Fridays.

A short distance ahead is the starting point for Don Lulo's popular 12km (7.5 miles) horseback tour to scenic **Nauyaca Falls** ❷ (http://nauyacawaterfalls-costarica.com; tel: 2787-0541; Mon–Sat at 8am). If you're not keen on horses, you can ride to these impressive falls in an open truck. Breakfast and lunch are provided; bring a swimsuit to enjoy the waterfall's natural pool. Make reservations at least one day in advance.

Just before you reach the Pacific coast you may be a little startled to see a Boeing 707 airplane fuselage parked on the left side of the road. This is the quite unusual **Gate One Charter Restaurant** (see ❶). There's a cocktail bar in the airplane for adults and a swimming pool for kids.

HACIENDA BARÚ WILDLIFE REFUGE

Route 243 ends at the intersection with Route 34, popularly called the Costanera Highway. Turning right (north) for 3km (2 miles) takes you to the **Hacienda Barú National Wildlife Refuge** ❸ (www.haciendabaru.com; daily 7am–7pm for tours), with 8km (5 miles) of trails through 330 hectares (815 acres) of wetlands, lowland tropical forest, and primary rain forest. Get a map at the office and walk the trails on your own or take a tour with a naturalist guide (5 hours). For a thrill, zip through the treetops on **The Flight of the Toucan canopy tour** or test yourself on the Monkey Challenge rope and obstacle course. Book a family-style cabin or comfortable modern room by the pool (see page 110) to get an early-morning jump on birds and wildlife.

DOMINICAL

Turning left at the intersection of routes 234 and the Costanera takes you across the Barú River bridge. Turn right immediately after the bridge, down the steep dirt road into 'downtown' **Dominical** ❹, basically a dusty, one-street affair. Park in front of **Pueblo del Río**, a 'village' of casual, open-air eateries, ranging from sushi, through vegan and organic foods, to fish and chips. The fish tacos at **El Pescado Loco** (see ❷) are hard to beat.

Follow the dusty main street south past the school and church and turn right to reach **Dominical Beach** ❺. A daily crafts and souvenir market under the palms has colorful sarongs waving in the ocean breezes. Sip refreshing

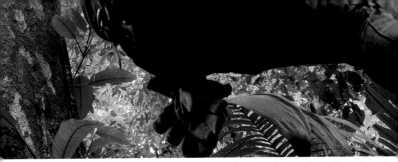

Getting ready to zip-line at Hacienda Barú

pipa (green coconut) juice with a straw inserted into the shell. This is primarily a surfing beach but if you want to swim in the Pacific, stay within the relatively safe area marked by flags, where lifeguards are on duty.

Dominicalito Beach

A mile or so farther south on the Costanera, watch for the Dominicalito sign and turn right on the dirt road across from the soccer field to **Dominicalito Beach 6**. This wide stretch, shaded by overhanging

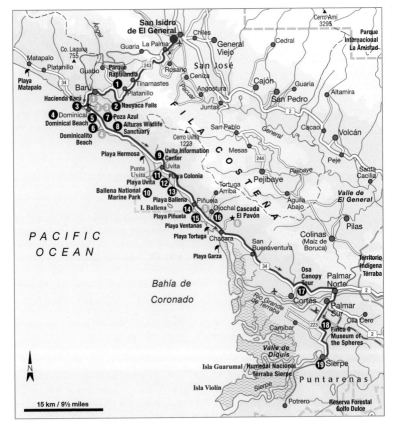

PACIFIC OCEAN

Bahía de Coronado

15 km / 9½ miles

A bird's-eye view of Uvita

beach almond trees, is perfect for beach-combing at low tide, with calm waters for swimming. Aside from Easter and Christmas, when locals pitch tents in the trees at the beach entrance, you may have the beach to yourself, especially early in the morning. Sunsets, if you walk north along the beach, are exquisite. An offshore, tree-topped rocky island silhouetted against the sun makes a stunning photograph.

For a refreshing dip without waves, turn left at the Dominicalito soccer field and follow the dirt road through a shallow stream and keep left uphill about 400 meters/yds to **Poza Azul** ❼. It's a short but steep hike down to a perfect, tree-shaded, clear pool at the base of a small waterfall. There's even a homemade Tarzan swing to launch yourself into the water. As always, do not leave any valuables in your car.

Another mile south on the Costanera, look on the right for the sign signaling the winding dirt road up to **La Parcela** (see ❻), an idyllic, open-air restaurant perched on a breezy headland jutting out into the Pacific, with splendid views up and down the coast.

ALTURAS WILDLIFE SANCTUARY

About 2km (3 miles) farther south on the Costanera, you can get close to wildlife at **Alturas Wildlife Sanctuary** ❽ (alturaswildlifesanctuary.org; tel: 2200-5440), a nonprofit rehabilitation center for rescued local creatures, including sloths, coatis, anteaters, monkeys, and

an odd kinkajou or two. Volunteers lead 90-minute tours (charge), four times daily except Monday. Reservations are a must and a 4X4 vehicle is definitely needed to climb the steep road.

UVITA

This is the major commercial hub along the coast, with banks, ATMs, super-markets, restaurants, stores, and a gas station lined up along the highway. The helpful **Uvita Information Center** ❾ (www.uvita.info), across from the BM Supermarket, has helpful advice and can book tours and accommodations. Next door is **Sibu Restaurant & Coffee Store** (tel: 2743-8674), a popular spot for excellent specialty coffees, craft beers, and notably sophisticated cakes and desserts.

Ballena National Marine Park

From Uvita, drive south on the Costanera over a bridge and turn right onto the road leading to the first entrance to **Ballena National Marine Park** ❿. Named for the humpback whales (ballenas) that visit from December through April, this park protects a swathe of coast stretching 10km (6 miles), with four separate beaches, from north to south: Uvita, Colonia, Ballena, and Piñuela.

Palm-fringed **Playa Uvita** ⓫ is the most popular beach, with a ranger station where you pay your entrance fee and pick up a map of the park. The access road is lined with restaurants

Having a whale of a time at the Ballena National Marine Park

and *cabinas* and there's paid parking just outside the entrance.

This beach is also the launching point for dolphin-watching, snorkeling, and fishing boat tours. Dolphin Tours of Bahía Ballena (www.dolphintourcostarica.com; tel: 2743-8013) is a reliable tour company.

At the north end of the park, there's a sandbar *(tombolo)* that at low tide resembles a whale's tail. When sunset and low tide coincide, it's a popular photographer's spot.

Each of the park entrances has a ranger station and basic restrooms and cold showers. Camping on the beach is permitted at **Playa Colonia** 🔢 2km (1.5 miles) south of Playa Uvita. **Playa Ballena** 🔢, about 3km (2 miles) farther south, has free parking, restrooms, cold showers, and BBQ pits. Pretty **Playa Piñuela** 🔢, set in a cove 3km (2 miles) farther south, has a pebbly beach but photogenic views of offshore islands.

Just south of the national park, **Playa Ventanas** 🔢 is a scenic, palm-shaded beach, backed by a forested mountain. Huge, offshore rock formations have window-like caves *(ventanas)* at low tide, popular with sea kayakers. Pineapple Tours in Dominical (www.pineapplekayaktours.com; tel: 8873-3283) can set you up with kayaks and paddleboards.

For a bird's-eye view of the coast and surrounding mountains, **Hotel Cristal Ballena** (see page 110) 7km (4.5 miles) south of Uvita, is a luxurious but affordable option, with the added advantage of the area's largest swimming pool.

OJOCHAL

Continuing south on the Costanera for 16km (10 miles) south of Uvita, you'll come to **Ojochal** 🔢, a mecca for gastronomes, first settled by French-Canadians who brought French culinary traditions with them. Right off the highway entrance, make the first left to a small commercial

---

Drake Bay Lodges

Sierpe is the launching point for boats to **Drake Bay lodges** and farther south along the Osa Pacific coast. Getting there is an adventure in itself. Boats meander along the Sierpe River, exploring mangroves, then literally surf a wave out into the Pacific Ocean at the river's mouth. In Drake Bay, romantic **La Paloma Lodge** (see page 111) and family-friendly **Drake Bay Wilderness** (see page 111) are all-inclusive lodges overlooking the Pacific. Farther south along the coast, comfortable **Casa Corcovado** (see page 110) is an off-the-grid eco-lodge that can still only be reached by boat, right on the northern border of Corcovado National Park and a short boat ride from **Isla del Caño**, famous for its snorkeling reef and thrilling dive spots. The 3km (2-mile) **Coastal Path** from Drake Bay to the **Río Claro Wildlife Refuge** is an unforgettable, scenic hiking trail cutting between dense jungle on the land side and crashing Pacific surf, with deserted sandy coves and beaches along the way and scarlet macaws overhead.

Drake Bay hills

plaza. Follow the aroma of baking bread to **Pancito Café** (closed Sun), a French bakery and casual terrace restaurant, offering light French fare for breakfast and lunch.

For more sophisticated French fusion fare, head next door to **Citrus Restaurante & Tapas** (see ④).

TILAPIAS EL PAVÓN

For an authentic Tico experience, continue south on the Costanera 3km (2 miles) and turn left, just past the yellow bus stop signed Punta Mala. Follow this winding dirt road uphill, along a scenic river for 4km (2.5 miles), heading to **Tilapias El Pavón** (see ⑤) in the tiny community of Vergel.

While the chef cooks your tilapia freshly caught from the adjoining fishpond, take a short hike along a forest path to view the nearby waterfall. The bird-watching is excellent here, either at the waterfall or around the prettily landscaped restaurant.

Less than a mile up the road, **Río Tico Safari Lodge** (see page 110) is an adventure in itself, with safari tents fixed on wood platforms perched over a rushing river.

OSA CANOPY

Continuing south on the Costanera, look for the **Osa Canopy Tour office** ⑰ (www.osacanopytour.com; tel: 2788-7555) at Km 196, 20km (12 miles) south of Uvita. If you haven't experienced a canopy adventure, this is an excellent chance to fly through the air along 3km (2 miles) of cable, launching yourself from 14 plat-

forms. The tour lasts two to three hours and includes rappelling and a Tarzan swing for the most adventurous zip-liners.

FINCA 6 MUSEUM OF THE SPHERES

For a rare insight into pre-Columbian culture in Costa Rica, continue south 45km (28 miles) to the turnoff on the right for **Palmar Sur**. Head west on the wide, flat road to Sierpe for 8km (5 miles).

En route, you'll pass vast tracts of African oil palm trees, interspersed with banana plantations, formerly owned by the United Fruit Company, which had its origin in Costa Rica, but pulled out after a labor dispute in the 1950s. You'll pass by small communities, still known by their *finca* (farm) numbers, with vintage two-story, wood *bananero* (banana workers) houses arranged around a central soccer field and a small church.

Watch for a sign on the left for **Finca 6 Museum of the Spheres** ⑱ (tel: 2100-6000; Tue–Sun 8am–4pm), just before a small bridge. This small but intriguing archeological museum details the history of massive stone spheres, dating from AD 800 to 1500, first uncovered by banana workers in the 1930s. Now a Unesco World Heritage Site, the modern museum has informative displays and pre-Columbian artifacts, along with trails to archeological sites where some spheres are still half-buried in the earth. The trails are hot and sunny, so bring a hat, plus binoculars and camera to spot birds and monkeys.

Rain forest canopy crab (or tree-climbing crab), Drake Bay

SIERPE

Another 5km (3 miles) south brings you to **Sierpe** ⑲, the end of the road and the jumping-off point for boats to Drake Bay eco-lodges and for tours in the largest mangrove in Central America. Naturalist guides and boat captains with sharp eyes pick out resident birds, monkeys, iguanas, crocodiles, and caimans along the way and delve deep into the mangrove to explain the ecology of this natural water filtration system. **Kokopelli Tours** (tel: 2788-1259; http://sierpemangrovetour.com) has an English-speaking guide; minimum two visitors.

Food and Drink

① GATE ONE CHARTER RESTAURANT

Route 34, 500 meters/yds north of Dominical; tel: 8542-5000/2787-0172; daily 11am–10.30pm; $$
The extensive menu at this lively, open-air eatery runs from burgers to more sophisticated pastas and seafood dishes. Portions are large enough to share. For fun, enjoy a cocktail and spicy chicken wings in the 727 fuselage.

② EL PESCADO LOCO

Pueblo del Río, Main Street, Dominical; tel: 8303-9042; daily 11.30am–7pm; $
Fresh local fish or shrimp, beer-battered and served with hand-cut fries, and spicy fish tacos served in a soft tortilla shell with guacamole are the main attractions here. For the more health conscious, there's also grilled fish.

③ LA PARCELA

Off Costanera Highway, 4km (2.5 miles) south of Dominical; tel: 2787-0016; www.laparcelacr.com; daily 11am–9pm; $$
Come for the view and feast on fresh seafood, from seafood soup to spaghetti marinara to grilled tuna with wasabi, accompanied by a glass of wine. Chicken choices and Mexican dishes will keep non-fish eaters happy.

④ CITRUS RESTAURANTE & TAPAS

Entrance to Ojochal; tel: 2786-5175; Mon, Tue 5–10pm, Wed–Sat noon–10pm, closed Sun; $$
Sophisticated world fare fused with French culinary skill, and served in a riverside setting make this the most exciting restaurant on the coast. Appetizers can make a meal, from *escargots* in garlic and blue cheese sauce to gingery Vietnamese shrimp *nems*. Save room for the standout Choco-Choco dessert.

⑤ TILAPIAS EL PAVÓN

Vergel de Punta Mala, 4km (2.5 miles) north from Km 179 on the Costanera Highway; tel: 2200-4721; Mon–Fri 9am–6pm, Sat–Sun 9am–8pm; $ (no credit cards)
Tico home-style cooking is at its best here. Order freshly caught tilapia whole or filleted, fried or grilled, accompanied by a heaping plate of rice, salad, fried yucca, and *patacones* (fried, mashed plantains). Wash it all down with local beer or a jug of fruit juice.

Life's a beach in Puerto Jiménez

OSA PENINSULA

This wildly scenic drive takes you off the grid, through a landscape uncluttered by utility poles and wires. You'll drive across narrow bridges and cross rivers as the road winds through lush tropical forest and culminates in the crashing surf of the Pacific Ocean.

DISTANCE: 88km (55 miles) round trip

TIME FULL DAY WITH STOPS, TWO TO THREE DAYS IF YOU PLAN TO STAY OVERNIGHT.

START: Puerto Jiménez

END: Carate

POINTS TO NOTE: You can fly to Puerto Jiménez from San José and rent a car for this drive. For most of the road, a 4X4 vehicle is not necessary; but you do need a 4X4 to access some lodges. Do not attempt this drive during the rainy season, September through December, when the rivers can run high and the road is muddy. Make sure you have enough fuel in your tank since there is none available south of Puerto Jiménez. If you choose to swim, watch out for concentrations of pebbles on the beach indicating a dangerous rip current.

Starting from Puerto Jiménez, the Osa Peninsula's last outpost of modern conveniences, the *lastre* road – a combination of gravel and hard dirt – hugs the east coast of the peninsula, which juts out more than 50km (30 miles) into the Pacific Ocean. This is the last, drivable, off-the-grid road in Costa Rica, unbroken by most of the sounds of modern civilization.

The road starts out fairly straight and flat, then winds upward through dense tropical forest. After crossing a dozen or so bridges and three rivers, you literally come to the end of the road at Playa Carate, pounded by Pacific Ocean waves.

This is prime eco-lodge territory, home to some of the country's most famous lodges. Scarlet macaws can almost always be heard overhead and seen on the beaches, feasting on beach almond tree nuts. Toucans are common, as are troops of monkeys and coatimundis crossing the road. So drive with caution and keep your windows open to hear the call of the wild.

PUERTO JIMÉNEZ

A dusty town with one main street, Puerto Jiménez looks a little like an

Chestnut-mandibled toucan

Boats moored in Puerto Jiménez

Old West frontier town, with scarlet macaws chattering in the trees instead of buzzards. The main attraction is the harbor front, with views across the sparkling Golfo Dulce, a tropical fjord, to the mainland.

The best place to stay in town and get reliable tourist information is at **Cabinas Jiménez** (see page 111), on the waterfront at the entrance to town, with modest but comfortable, air-conditioned rooms. Just a short walk away is cheerful **Mail It Pizza**

(see ❶), the town's best Italian restaurant. A more luxurious beachfront option is **Iguana Lodge** (see page 111) set in a lush tropical estate fronting **Playa Platanares** ❶, 11km (7 miles) southeast of town. Iguana Lodge also has the most upscale and romantic restaurant, **La Perla de Osa** (see ❷), on a breezy terrace with a view of the Golfo.

If bird-watching is on your agenda, the best birding and guide are 12km (7.5 miles) west of town at **Bosque del**

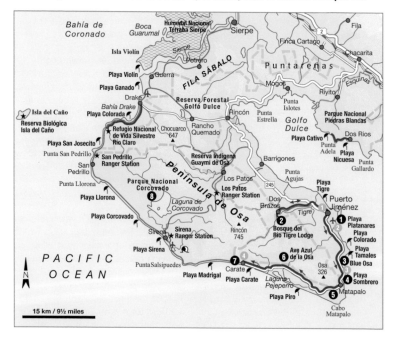

Golfo Dulce

Río Tigre Lodge ❷ (bosquedelriotigre.com), one of the top three birding hotspots in the country.

ON THE ROAD

On the main street in Puerto Jiménez, drive south past the church and turn right at the gas station, then follow the signs for **Carate** via Route 245. Be sure your gas tank is at least half full since there is no fuel between here and Carate.

In about 2.5km (1.5 miles) you'll come to the first of 11 narrow bridges. If there's no traffic, take a moment to pause and check for birds along the stream below. Ibis, herons, kingfishers, and egrets are often spotted in the streams along the road.

Jagua Arts & Crafts

If you're in the shopping mood, head to **Jagua Arts & Crafts**, located beside the Puerto Jiménez airfield. This is the Southern Zone's finest and most sophisticated collection of hand-crafted gifts and souvenirs, from indigenous carved masks to exquisite glass-bead jewelry to a wide selection of natural-history field guides, plus organic chocolate and cups of exotic-flavored Jade Luna ice cream for those looking for a sweet treat. It opens early, at 6.30am, to catch passengers on early flight departures.

After a few more kilometers, the overhead electrical wires disappear and you are officially off the grid and in the land of gaunt, white Brahman cattle, grazing in pastures backed by forested hills to the east and fenced in by lines of gumbo lindo trees.

GOLFO DULCE

Beyond the fourth bridge, the view on the left opens up to the panoramic scenery of the shimmering Golfo Dulce and the mist-shrouded mainland to the west. As the heat rises, you'll see cattle gathering under the cool canopy of wide-spreading trees.

Most of the shoreline along the road is inaccessible, fronted by private property, but you can get a glimpse of beach by stopping in at **Blue Osa ❸**, a lush, landscaped yoga retreat. Order a fruit drink and take a stroll down to the shore. Or continue another 4km (2.5 miles) along the road, looking on the left for a large tree trunk painted with an arrow pointing to a soft dirt road. Follow the road 30 meters/yds or so to **Playa Sombrero ❹**, a long stretch of mostly deserted beach. You can park under a palm and enjoy the breezy view, but swim with caution since rip currents can be dangerous here.

Another 2km (1.2 miles) south is the only refreshment stop on this half of the road. **Martina's** (see ❸), formerly known as Bar Buena Esperanza, hops on Friday nights with din-

Playa Pan Dulce, Matapalo　　　　　　　　*A forest walk in El Remanso*

ner and DJ music till midnight. Friday mornings there's an artisan market featuring local crafts and foods, most notably tubs of handmade Jade Luna ice cream from Puerto Jiménez. Every day, there's breakfast and a healthy lunch menu focused on fresh fish.

MATAPALO AND ITS ECO-LODGES

Some 500 meters/yds on is one of the deeper river crossings, over the **Río Carbonera**, dangerous in rainy season, but easily passable in dry season thanks to a stony bottom. From here, the road begins its climb up into dense tropical forest.

You are now officially in **Matapalo ❺**. Look for a steep dirt road going down on the left, leading to a scattering of beach houses. Park on the main road – be sure to lock up and take any valuables with you – and take a stroll down to Playa Pan Dulce, a popular surfing beach. This stretch of rough road is also popular with birding and wildlife tours, so bring binoculars and cameras.

Back on the main road, just a little farther along on the right, you'll see the steep entrance to **Lapa Ríos** (see page 112), the first and foremost eco-lodge in the country. It's worth a call ahead to reserve for lunch here in the Brisa Azul restaurant. The food is excellent and the views from the ridge-top lodge are spectacular.

The road continues to wind upward and the forest gets denser. A mile

beyond Lapa Ríos, on the left is the entrance to **Bosque del Cabo** (see page 111), another notable eco-lodge with artistically luxurious bungalows and excellent trails and guided wildlife tours. You are free to drive in and park at reception to check out the lodge for future reference.

Almost next door is the entrance to **El Remanso** (see page 112), famous for its thrilling waterfall rappelling tour. You can call ahead to reserve a spot if the tour isn't already filled with lodge guests. The romantic terrace dining room here, set under palm trees, can also be reserved by non-guests for lunch or dinner.

RÍO PIRRO

The road continues wending through forest and slowly starts to descend to the **Río Pirro** (one of the widest rivers along the road, but usually shallow enough to cross easily.

The road opens up again with pastures on both sides, and more cattle and horses at home on the range. A few kilometers along, look for a sign on the right for **Ave Azul de la Osa ❻** (www.aveazuldelaosa.com; daily 9am–4pm), a breeding farm for endangered bird species with a small natural history museum and 15km (9 miles) of hiking trails. This is your chance to have your photo taken with a non-native hyacinth macaw or kookaburra.

Getting that perfect shot at sunrise in Carate

The only other refreshment stop along the road is rustic bar/restaurant **Bijagual**, offering cold beer and fruit drinks and Costa Rican *comida típica*, from 5am till sunset.

CARATE

Approaching **Carate** ❼, the road suddenly winds precipitously down to sea level. Bamboo and vine-draped trees form a roof over the road and you can see and smell the ocean on the left.

Watch for a side road signed Shady Lane, and turn right to visit the village's attractive modern school, built entirely of bamboo.

You can't miss the signs for **Lookout Inn** (see ❹), a hilltop lodge famous for its margaritas and sunset bar with views of the coast stretching for miles. Stop in for refreshment and a chance to see scarlet macaws from bird's-eye level, feasting on the beachfront almond trees below. A troop of *titi* (squirrel) monkeys also visits, enticed by free bananas. Non-guests can also reserve a table for the nightly BBQ buffet.

The beach is public and there are plenty of places to park under shade trees, but the surf is pretty wild. It's best to check with locals about the safe times for swimming.

The last lodge on the road is **Finca Exotica** (see page 112), an all-inclusive organic farm, exquisite garden, and eco-lodge with a choice of plat-

form tents or Indonesian-style Tiki cabins.

Route 245 ends at the airstrip, where small charter planes ferry visitors to nearby **Corcovado National Park**. From here, it's a 45-minute walk along the beach to the La Leona entrance to the park. If you have made a reservation with a guide for a tour in the park, you can leave your car in the parking lot at the rustic Carate soda restaurant ($5 per night); the café also has basic restrooms. This is also the last stop on the road, where taxis and a *colectivo* truck-taxi drop off and pick up visitors to the national park.

CORCOVADO NATIONAL PARK

For decades, the call of the wild Osa has come from **Corcovado National Park** ❽, the jewel in the crown of the national park system. It's still Central America's largest tract of lowland rain forest, home to sought-after wildlife and birds, including rarely seen tapirs and jaguars. But gone are the days when you could pay a daily fee and hike into the park on your own, or set up a tent at a ranger station.

Now, you must reserve no more than a month in advance, book and pay for lodging in bunk beds on covered platforms and for your meals and hire a licensed guide. Agencies in Puerto Jiménez can do all this for you – the eco-mindful Osa Wild (tel: 2735-5848; www.osawildtravel.com)

Corcovado cascades

can arrange a three-day, two-night park visit for about $460 per person (minimum two people).

You can also make park reservations by e-mailing pncorcovado@gmail.com. Once you have a paid receipt, you can arrange for food and lodging through the non-profit Asociación de Desarrollo Integral de Corcovado de Carate (reservaciones@adicorcovado.org). Even if you don't intend to spend a night in the park, you still have to hire a guide to walk the trails. For a reliable day guide, e-mail the Asociación de Guías de Puerto Jiménez (aguilosacr@gmail.com).

A very rough road, traveling along the Río Carate riverbed and up a steep mountain definitely requires a sturdy 4X4 vehicle with high clearance. The destination is mountaintop Luna Lodge (see page 112), a legend among yoga enthusiasts and bird-watchers.

Food and Drink

① MAIL IT PIZZA

Across from the soccer field on the main street; tel: 2735-5483; daily 4–10.30pm, closed Tue in low season; $

Upbeat Italian cooks from Trieste make authentic crisp-crust pizzas and tasty homemade pastas in this cheerful restaurant, formerly the post office. Eat in or enjoy your meal sitting by the side of the bay.

② LA PERLA DE OSA

Iguana Lodge, Playa Platanares, 5km (3 miles) south of the airfield; tel: 8848-0752; iguanalodge.com; daily 11am–8.30pm; $$

For romantic dining, nothing beats this open-air restaurant cooled by gulf breezes, serving sophisticated fare that fuses Asian, Mexican, Mediterranean, and tropical flavors. The four-soup starter can be a meal in itself and the fresh seafood dishes are exceptional. Save room for the deservedly famous brownie with homemade ice cream.

③ MARTINA'S BAR & RESTAURANT

On Rte. 245, just before Río Carbonera crossing, near Matapalo; no phone; daily 9am–9pm, Fri until 1am; $$

Formerly known as Bar Esperanza, the only upscale roadside restaurant on the Osa Peninsula is a winner. Friday nights are especially lively with music till late in the evening at this breezy, art-filled outdoor space. The menu changes daily, featuring fresh tuna, mahi-mahi, chicken, vegetarian salads and pastas, and a wide choice of beer, fruit cocktails, and wine.

④ LOOKOUT INN

Facing the beach in Carate; reserve by e-mail terry@lookout–inn.com; lunch at noon, dinner at 6.30pm; $$$

The place for sunset drinks, with views along the coast and almost guaranteed sightings of scarlet macaw pairs flying to nearby roosts. Dinner features BBQ buffets in a crow's-nest loft and may include visits by begging *titi* (squirrel) monkeys.

Arenal Volcano rising from the plain is an unforgettable sight

ARENAL

Just about every tour of Costa Rica includes a quick visit to Arenal, to soak in hot springs with a view of the iconic, perfectly cone-shaped Arenal Volcano. Aside from a plethora of adrenaline-rushing adventure parks, there's also a naturally wild side around Lake Arenal that is worth exploring at a more leisurely pace.

DISTANCE: 183km (114 miles)
TIME: At least two days with activities
START: Juan Santamaría Airport, San José
END: Tilarán
POINTS TO NOTE: Start out early to get ahead of traffic and take it slow on the misty road above San Ramón. Bring a bathing suit, hiking shoes, binoculars, and your camera. The best season to see Arenal Volcano, which is often hidden by clouds, is the dry season, December through April, early morning and late afternoon. From Tilarán, you can make connections to Monteverde, 71km (44 miles) south via the Inter-Americana Highway; or to the Nicoya Peninsula via the Friendship Bridge across the Río Tempisque, 75km (46.5 miles) south.

Arenal Volcano is a relative newcomer on the geological scene. The sudden, spectacular eruption in July 1968 not only gave rise to a 1,670-meter (5,479ft) -high volcano suddenly looming over the plain, but also to an explosion of tourist development.

Since 2010 the volcano has been dormant and the pyrotechnical shows of red lava are over for now, but the town of La Fortuna is still a hotbed of bars, restaurants, souvenir shops, and tour agencies.

For a calmer option, head west along the shores of Lake Arenal, a 35km- (22-mile) long lake created in 1973 when the natural valley with a low lake was flooded to create a huge hydroelectric project. On a clear day, the best views of Arenal Volcano are from the far western end of the lake.

The most scenic drive from San José is via San Ramón, along a mountain road up and over a cloud forest, down to La Fortuna.

SAN JOSÉ TO LA FORTUNA

Drive north along the Inter-American Highway from Juan Santamaría Airport, heading to San Ramón, 43km (27 miles) away. About 13km (8 miles) past the airport, the highway curves and an iconic Costa Rican view opens up: fields of waving, wheat-colored sugar-cane plumes, interspersed with the dark-green leaves of coffee plantations. On the horizon, the soft green of the volcanic ridge of **Juan Castro Blanco**

Exploring on horseback

National Park rises up, blanketed by white clouds and blue sky above.

A little farther along, on the right, you'll pass the Cacique factory. This is the largest distiller of *guaro*, Costa Rica's national liquor, made from all that sugar cane.

The road climbs, thankfully with some passing lanes, to the exit for San Ramón. Follow this one-way road straight through town, passing the huge, white cathedral on your left. A few blocks on, this road curves left one block, to a traffic light. Turn right at the light and follow the road north, past the hospital. You will come to a T-junction recognizable by a church decorated with angels. Go left on Route 702, following the sign to La Fortuna, 63km (39 miles) away .

LOS ANGELES CLOUD FOREST

The road quickly leaves the city behind and winds up into the clouds, passing coffee and banana plantations, followed by pastures grazed by white, hump-backed Brahman cows, which produce the milk for the fresh cheese sold in small stores along the road.

Approaching the small village of Angeles Norte, look for the sign on the right to **Villa Blanca Cloud Forest Hotel & Nature Reserve ❶** (see page 114). Literally in the clouds, this upscale hotel has guided naturalist tours through a private preserve.

ON THE WAY UP

The road continues up for the next 12km (7.5 miles) past variegated-green hill-sides studded with the plants you usually see decorating offices. These are *follaje verde* (green foliage) ornamental plant farms, with acres of dracaenas destined for export. The netted-over areas are protecting ferns from too much sun, until they are also exported around the world.

The 'Neblina' road signs warn of fog, so go slow. When you reach the DRACA fern farm, the road starts a slow, winding descent, passing over rushing rivers, mostly on narrow, one-way bridges. Be sure to slow down and yield to oncoming vehicles.

Bungee jumping

If you aren't already getting an adrenaline rush from driving across the bridges, watch out for **Eco-Bungee ❷** (tel: 8344-0123; daily 8am–4pm), just past the Río La Cataratita bridge. Their slogan '*Adrenalina pura*' needs no translation. Here's your chance to jump off a 100-meter (328ft) -high suspension bridge into a cloud forest ravine. Or you can simply walk over the suspension bridge, hike a trail, and visit a butterfly enclosure.

Lands in Love

Another 12km (7.5 miles) on, hemmed in by dense cloud forest, the road reaches **Lands in Love Restaurant** (see ❶).

ON THE WAY DOWN

There are a few more bridges to cross as you slowly wind down. At Baja Rodriguez, keep left, following the sign to La Tigra.

Iguana taking it easy in Los Angeles Cloud Forest

Along the road, it's worth stopping at **San Lorenzo Recycled Art** ❸ near **Valle Azul** for its collection of recycled tires cleverly fashioned into exotic birds and animals by a local artisan.

When you reach La Tigra, turn left at the soccer field, following the sign for Javillos, then keep right, still on Route 702. About 7km (4.3 miles) on, you come to the Río Peñas Bridge, the high-

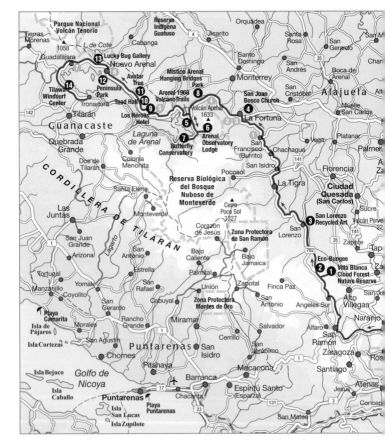

San Juan Bosco Church on a misty day

est, single-lane, slightly rickety suspension bridge along this route.

At El Bosque, the road finally starts to straighten out, replacing cloud forest with pastures and a teasing glimpse or two of the volcano. Just after crossing the Río Burro, if you're in luck, on a clear day you will see Arenal Volcano looming ahead.

In San Francisco, 8km (5 miles) south of La Fortuna, **El Gran Abuelo Parrillada y Restaurant** (see ❷) is a great steak-lunch option.

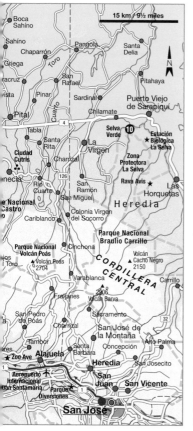

LA FORTUNA

Route 702 segues into the bustling, commercial heart of **La Fortuna**. Straight ahead is **San Juan Bosco Church** ❹ probably the most photographed church in Costa Rica, providing foreground interest for photos of the distant volcano, due west. Behind the church Desafio Adventure Company (tel: 2479-0020; www.desafiocostarica.com) specialises in any adventure on the water, including rafting, paddling, and waterfall rappelling.

Turn left, just before the church, onto Route 142, the cluttered main road that leads west to hotels, restaurants, hot springs, adventure parks, and Lake Arenal. If you didn't get lunch earlier, try **La Choza de Laurel** (see ❸), a Tico-style, open-air restaurant with large portions of *comida típica*.

VOLCANO ROAD

For the next 15km (9 miles) or so, the road passes by an almost uninterrupted string of hotels, restaurants, adventure parks, and hot spring resorts, all oriented toward the volcano, which dominates the south (left) side of the road.

The one restaurant not to miss along this road is the elegant **Que Rico** (see ❹), with perhaps the best, close-up volcano view.

Among the many hotels lining this road, some with their own private thermal springs, two places almost side-by-side share the same volcano view, but with very different styles and prices. The budget choice is charming **Cabinas Los Guayabos** (see page 114), right next door to the deluxe, pricey **Arenal Kioro Suites & Spa** (see page 114).

Caño Negro Refuge

Covering 96 sq km (38 sq miles) this wet, lowland rain-forest preserve, home to caimans, crocodiles, turtles, and over 300 resident and migratory bird species, is a must-see for birders and wildlife-watchers. The best way to view it is from a boat with a naturalist guide, from November through March, gliding over the seasonal lake that forms after the rainy season. It's a two-hour drive north of La Fortuna toward Los Chiles, on mostly paved roads with a bumpy dirt road for the final 19km (12 miles). You need to set out onto the lake early, so it's best to reserve a room the night before at **Natural Lodge Caño Negro** (tel: 2471-1426; www.canonegrolodge.com), which runs early-morning boat tours with a bilingual guide. Advertised tours to Caño Negro from La Fortuna do not visit the actual preserve; their boat tours travel on the nearby Río Frío.

Birds and butterflies

About 6km (4 miles) past Tabacón Hot Springs, take a left turn to **El Castillo**. The wide, dirt road leads first to **Arenal 1968 Volcano Trails** ❺ (daily 8am–4pm; under 10s free), where you can set off on two different hiking trails. The 4km (2.5-mile) 'Lava Flow' hike gains 520 meters (1,700ft) of altitude for panoramic views from the volcano's original lava fields. The slightly longer, also steep, Forest Trail leads through rain forest and around a small lake. You'll find free parking, a trail map, a café, and restrooms at the park entrance.

Continue south on the dirt road to the entrance, on the left, for **Arenal Observatory Lodge** ❻ (see page 114), the premier lodge for bird-watchers and hikers – and the closest hotel to the volcano. Even if you don't stay here, you can buy a $10 pass giving you access to the lodge's trails (from 7am) and botanical gardens, and use of the restaurant, with panoramic views of the volcano and Lake Arenal.

The dirt road makes a right turn west along the scenic, southern edge of Lake Arenal to El Castillo, a small village with a café and small supermarket. Turn left at the sign for the **Butterfly Conservatory** ❼ (tel: 2479-1149; www.butterflyconservatory.org; under 6s free) and head up the hill. Here, over 1,000 butterflies, representing 35 species, live in six different tented habitats spread over 10 acres of regenerated rain forest. Start at the insect museum and Puparium, where about 75 butterflies a day emerge from their cocoons. Bilingual guides assist visitors along the way.

Enjoying the clear, fresh water of the Cataratas del Río Fortuna

Retrace your route back to Route 142 and turn left, heading west. Just before the Lake Arenal dam, is the entrance to **Mistico Arenal Hanging Bridges Park** ❽ (tel: 2479-8282; https://misticopark.com; daily 7.30am–4.30pm). This one-stop adventure park has trails over 16 suspension bridges, horseback rides, a zip-line, and more extreme sports such as 'zorbing' in a plastic sphere down a steep hill, canyoning, and waterfall rappelling. There are also calmer birding, natural history, and night-walk tours.

LAKE ARENAL

Route 142 runs right across the dam that holds in Lake Arenal at its eastern end. Drive over the dam and from here on, the paved road meanders between forested hills and the lake, glimpsed through the lush greenery. Past the entrance to Arenal Lodge, watch out for coatimundis crossing the road or looking for handouts. It's fine to stop and take photos from your car but do not feed the animals and do not get close as coatis bite.

The best way to see the lake is out on the water. **Arenal Kayaks** (tel: 2694-4336; http://arenalkayaks.com) offers guided, two-hour tours, setting off from a dock 4km (2.5 miles) west of the dam.

LITTLE SWITZERLAND

The tropical forest suddenly gives way, about 10km (6.2 miles) farther on, to Little Switzerland. **Los Héroes Restau-**rant & Hotel ❾ (tel: 2692-8012; www.pequenahelvecia.com) is a quaint property, with scattered Swiss chalets, an Alpine chapel, brown cows grazing in pastures and a two-car electric train that takes visitors on an hour-long tour up to a mirador for lunch or coffee. The main **restaurant** (see ❺) serves great alpine fare.

LA UNION

For one of the best – and cheapest – rooms with a view of the lake, visit hilltop **Arenal Volcano Lake Lodge** (see page 114), beside the church in the small community of La Union, 10km

Hot Springs

About 5km (3.2 miles) west of La Fortuna are a cluster of hot springs practically side by side: **EcoTermales Fortuna** (http://ecotermalesfortuna.cr) and **Kalambu Hot Springs Water Park** (www.kalambu.com), and across the road, **Baldi Hot Springs** (www.baldihotsprings.cr). Pick the atmosphere that suits you best – Kalambu and Baldi feature slides and play areas for children, while EcoTermales is more romantic, especially in the evenings. Prices range from $32 to $40 for adults, around $25 for kids, with package prices that include meals. The most famous hot spring is 4km (2.5 miles) farther west, the deluxe **Grand Spa at Tabacón** (www.tabacon.com). Prices here start at $70 adults/$25 children, and reservations are required.

Tour boats on Lake Arenal

(6.2 miles) east of Nuevo Arenal. The recently renovated rooms are charming, with painted wildlife murals and king-size beds, or family rooms with bunks and single beds. The hotel's **Restaurante Alondra** has delicious, savory *bocas* (appetizers), big enough to share while gazing out over the lake.

Just down the road at **Toad Hall** (tel: 2692-8181; toadhallhotel.com), on the restaurant terrace, order a cocktail and enjoy another great lake view.

You can't miss the fluorescent green sign for **Avatar Tree** , signaling the start of a steepish hike up to a majestic 500-year-old ceiba (kapok) tree, covered in vines and epiphytes. Stretch your legs, learn a little local history and get a great view of the lake, all for $2.

NUEVO ARENAL

Approaching the town of **Nuevo Arenal** – 'new' because it replaced the previous town, which was in the flooded valley that is now Lake Arenal – is **Villa Decary** (see page 114) (tel: 2694-4330; www.villadecary.com), the best B&B on the lake, with views from five hilltop bungalows, set in a lush tropical forest with easy bird-watching.

The main road into town has a cluster of restaurants, notably the German Bakery. Almost next door **Los Platillos Voladores** (see ⑥) serves authentic Italian fare.

It's not easy to get waterfront access along the lakeshore, but the town's **Peninsula Park** , off a dirt road south of town, is a pleasant picnic and swimming spot.

Route 142, which becomes the town's main street, has a gas station, small supermarkets, and a pharmacy. The road then heads up inland.

WESTERN LAKE ARENAL

About 3km (2 miles) west of town stop in at **Lucky Bug Gallery** (daily 7am–3pm) for colorful ceramics, lamps, painted tiles, and unusual objets d'art. The friendly German owners also serve *bratwurst* and *schnitzels* at their **Caballo Negro** restaurant (tel: 2694-4515).

The road twists and winds past some upscale villa developments and a private marina. Just before the small town of Río Piedras, keep an eye out for **Café y Macadamia Restaurant** (see ⑦) with its divine cakes and bird's-eye view of the lake.

The western end of the lake is prime windsurfing territory. You can book a lesson with **Tilawa Windsurf Center** (tel: 8778-1492; costa-rica-windsurf.com), based in the Lake Arenal Hotel overlooking the windiest part of the lake.

A few kilometers on, Route 142 turns west, away from the lake, heading for Tilarán, 4km (2.5 miles) on. But just before the turn is the very best vantage point for viewing the entire length of the lake, with the volcano dead-center in the background.

From Tilarán, you can make connections to Monteverde, 71km (44 miles) south via the Inter-American Highway; or from here you can head southwest 75km (46.5 miles) south toward the Friendship Bridge, leading to the Nicoya Peninsula.

German charm at Los Héroes Hotel

Food and Drink

1 LANDS IN LOVE RESTAURANT
Road to La Fortuna, near San Lorenzo; tel: 2447-9331; https://landsinlove.com; daily 8am–3pm; $
This quirky Israeli vegan restaurant posts amusing signs along the road advertising its meatless burgers, dips and salads. Tasty homemade cookies and brownies.

2 EL GRAN ABUELO PARRILLADA Y RESTAURANTE
San Francisco, 8km (5 miles) south of La Fortuna; tel: 2479-1749; Tue–Sun noon–9pm; $$
This family-style rancho restaurant is one of the best local steakhouses. Large portions of tender, grilled-to-order steaks are served on sizzling skillets. Non meat-eaters will enjoy the ceviche and wood-fired veggie pizza. Save room for key lime cheesecake.

3 LA CHOZA DE LAUREL
Route 142, 400 meters/yds northwest of the church in La Fortuna; tel: 2479-7063; https://lachozadelaurel.com; daily 11am–10pm; $$
The aroma of roasting chickens at this open-air restaurant is irresistible. The extensive menu is both modern and *típico*. It's popular with tour groups, so come off-peak.

4 QUE RICO
6.5km (4 miles) west of La Fortuna on Route 142; tel: 2479-1020; www.quericoarenal.com; daily 11am–9.30pm; $$$

In a sophisticated decor with a volcano view, feast on a menu featuring Lebanese and other Mediterranean cuisines. But stick with Italian for dessert: Bacio Perugina, a pastry shell stuffed with Nutella and caramelized almonds.

5 LOS HÉROES RESTAURANT & HOTEL
Route 142, 9km (12 miles) west of La Fortuna; tel: 2692-8012; www.pequenahelvecia.com; breakfast 7–10am, lunch 11am–4pm, dinner 6–8.30pm; $$
For something different, dig into *wiener schnitzel*, *roësti* with a fried egg, Hungarian goulash, or a Veal Cordon Bleu at this Swiss chalet. Or go all out with an authentic cheese or meat fondue.

6 LOS PLATILLOS VOLADORES
Entrance road into Nuevo Arenal; tel: 2694-5005; Mon–Fri noon–3pm and 7–11pm, Sat 1–4pm and 7pm–midnight; $
Don't be fooled by the eccentric name (Flying Saucers), this is serious Italian food, cheerfully served by Emy from Verona. Husband David makes perfect pizzas and huge portions of pasta. Pasta al pesto with shrimp is a highlight. Drinks and wine are Italian, too.

7 CAFÉ Y MACADAMIA RESTAURANT
Route 142, 11km (7 miles) west of Nuevo Arenal; tel: 2448-0030; daily 8am–5pm; $$
Along with cakes and rolls, this bustling café with a lake view serves large platters of fish, chicken, or meat, accompanied by homemade focaccia and vegetable sides. The signature cappuccino is flavored with macadamia liqueur and topped with slivered nuts.

Monteverde coffee beans

MONTEVERDE

Famous for pristine, primeval cloud forests filled with wildlife, the Monteverde area is a mecca for nature lovers. New restaurants, hotels, and high-adrenaline adventure parks have increased the tourist crowds, but it's still possible to find yourself alone in a mist-enshrouded forest.

DISTANCE: 5 to 8km (3 to 5 miles), depending on side trips
TIME: 1 full day walking; 2 days with stops and visits
START: Santa Elena
END: Monteverde Reserve
POINTS TO NOTE: You could easily walk from Santa Elena to the Monteverde Reserve in a day. But if you want to stop along the way, allow at least two days.

It's not easy to get here, and that's the way the locals want to keep it, to avoid being overrun by day-trippers. But once you arrive – either by car, private shuttle van, or public bus – you can actually get around the old-fashioned way: on foot.

Many of the best natural attractions, lodges, and restaurants, are accessible along the 3km (2-mile) stretch of mostly paved road between the center of Santa Elena and the Monteverde Cheese Factory. Taxis, shuttle vans, and public buses can get you to the farther nature preserves, where the only way to tour is on foot. Just about every outlying adventure park provides transportation from your lodge.

Along with nature, Monteverde is famous for cheese and ice cream, along with coffee and chocolate tours and tastings. So lace up your hiking boots and explore while earning calories to spend at tempting local eateries

SANTA ELENA

Start at the **Chamber of Tourism ❶** office on Santa Elena's main street to pick up a local map and browse the racks of tour brochures touting canopy tours, hanging bridges, horseback rides, and coffee tours.

Walk south on the main street toward the Banco Nacional. Turn the corner (left) past the bank and the entrance to **Arco Iris Lodge** (see page 115), an unusual country lodge in the town.

A few steps farther on, you reach the **Jardín de Orquídeas ❷** (Orchid Garden; tel: 2645-5308; daily 8am–5pm), where more than 450 species of orchids bloom throughout the year, with 120 or so in bloom at any one time. Take a 30-minute informative tour and

Orchid Garden bloom

Just hatched at the Butterfly Farm

then roam on your own, equipped with a jeweler's loupe that allows you to peer at even the most miniature specimens.

Next door to the garden is the artsy, vegetarian-friendly **Orchid Coffee Shop** (see ①), with 25 versions of local coffee and a $2 discount to the Orchid Garden.

CERRO PLANO

Continue south to the main road and turn left downhill, heading toward **Cerro Plano**, Santa Elena's close neighbor. Just before you reach the school, stop in at the **Monteverde ArtHouse** ❸ (tel: 2645-5275; daily 10am–6pm), set back from the road in a pretty garden. Even if you're not buying, browsing through these small rooms filled with brightly colored, one-of-a-kind ceramics, paintings, and textiles is pure pleasure.

At the school, turn right (west) down a dirt road to **De Lucia** (see ②), a South American restaurant, noted for its steaks, fresh fish, and friendly Chilean host.

THE BUTTERFLY FARM

Continue walking along this road 100 meters/yds or so until you see the sign for the **Butterfly Farm**. Turn left (south) down this road to the farm, also called **Jardín de Mariposas** ❹ (www.monteverdebutterfly garden.com; daily 8.30am–4pm). Engaging entomologists take you on a guided tour of the insect collection – kids will love handling giant beetles and releasing a just-emerged butterfly in one of the four enclosed habitats. You can sit in the garden enclosures amongst the butterflies, which are most active on sunny mornings. White-faced monkeys often make an appearance.

SUNSET SPOT

Retrace your steps to the main road and turn right (south), downhill, past the entrance to **Los Pinos** ❺ (see page 115), an 18-acre private preserve with cabins and an hydroponic vegetable garden.

On the west side of the road, a superb view opens up – as far as the Gulf of Nicoya on a clear day. Come back later to watch the sunset.

A berry-loving bat at the Bat Jungle

HOTEL BELMAR

Continue a couple of hundred meters/yds downhill, past the CPI language school and turn left at the gas station to climb the steep road to the luxury, chalet-style **Belmar Hotel** (see page 115), Monteverde's finest, fronted by a wide terrace with a commanding view westward. You can order drinks and superb bar food and take a seat on the terrace. Around sunset, 4.30pm to 5.30pm, come for drink specials and craft beers with free *bocas* (appetizers). For the most romantic dinner in town, reserve a table at the hotel's elegant restaurant, **Celajes** (see ❸).

BAT JUNGLE MONTEVERDE

Past the gas station, the paved road becomes a dirt road. Continue downhill about 400 meters/yds to the **Bat Jungle Monteverde** ❻ (tel: 2645-9999; daily 9am–6pm) for a very different natural experience. During this 45-minute tour you'll learn all about these often misunderstood creatures while observing more than 90 bats, representing eight species. On the wing in a simulated nocturnal jungle setting, the bats socialize, feed, nurse, and, on occasion, give birth.

After observing these creatures of the night, climb a stairway up to heavenly **Café Caburé Restaurant and Chocolate Shop** (see ❹), a chic, Argentine café with a terrace overlooking the Bat Jungle entrance. Along with savory South American cuisine, this restaurant is known for its selection of handmade chocolates and delectable desserts. Tours of their chocolate factory (charge), including tastings, are available daily by reservation.

Across the road is **Tramonti** (see ❺), a popular Italian restaurant overlooking a lush garden.

CASEM

Next door, at the entrance to **El Bosque Lodge** is a magnificent **fig tree ❼**, a landmark for bird-watchers. When the tree has fruit, you can sit on the nearby grass and observe a wide range of fruit-eating birds that come to feast on the red berries, along with the occasional monkey.

At the back of the grassy area lies the large showroom for **CASEM ❽** (Cooperativa de Artesania de Santa Elena y Monteverde; daily 7.30am–5pm). The embroidery work, leather goods, and handmade clothes here are a little old-fashioned but superb, especially the embroidered birds on dish towels. Hand-sewn hummingbirds and quetzals made of felt make great Christmas tree ornaments, and easy-to-pack souvenirs.

Next door to CASEM is **Café Monteverde ❾** (tel: 2645-7550; 7am–6pm) where you can sample four different styles of coffee before choosing your favorite. Sip your brew in the hip café, or take your cup out to the native plants garden behind the café, where there's a picnic table. You can also book a coffee tour here to the café's sustainable farm just 3km (2 miles) out of town.

Monteverde Cheese Factory

The Curi-Cancha Reserve is a hiker's paradise

Directly across the road from CASEM is a good, early-morning birding spot, on the back terrace of Stella's Bakery, which opens at 6.30am. Grab a cup of coffee and a pastry, and watch the birds fly in.

BAJO DEL TIGRE TRAIL

About 100 meters/yds south along the road, watch for the entrance on the left to the **Bajo del Tigre** sector ❿ of the vast **Children's Eternal Rainforest** (tel: 2645-5305; www.acmcr.org), a 218.5sq km (84.4 sq miles) forest preserve funded by children from 44 countries. Even though this section is relatively tiny, the 3.5 km (2 miles) of self-guided trails are varied and well-marked, with informative signposts along the way. It's usually very quiet along the wooded trails, with an excellent chance of spotting birds and small animals, such as coatis, agoutis, and monkeys. A children's house at the reception center is full of interactive exhibits. There's also a guided night tour, by reservation.

MONTEVERDE CHEESE FACTORY

Continue south to the **Monteverde Cheese Factory** ⓫ (tel: 2645-7090; Mon–Sat 7.30am–5pm, Sun 8am–4pm), the economic engine that underpinned Monteverde's founding by Quakers, who left the United States in the 1950s in protest over the Korean War. It's still churning out cheeses that are sold all over the country. But the main attraction here is ice cream and milkshakes whipped up in the café.

CURI-CANCHA RESERVE

To reach one of the best hiking areas, follow the road to the left (north side) of the Cheese Factory 300 meters/yds to the private **Curi-Cancha Reserve** ⓬ (tel: 2645-6915; https://reservacuricancha.com). The trails here are well maintained and easily manageable, cutting through cloud forest and wet lowlands, a meadow filled with *rabo de gato* (porterweed) bushes that attract hummingbirds, and a higher lookout with a view over the continental divide.

More than 200 species of birds have been recorded here, including quetzals, bellbirds, and trogons. The preserve's signature bird is the collared redstart, popularly known as *amigo de hombre* (man's friend), a bird that often accompanies people along a trail. Frequently sighted animals include coatis, agoutis, armadillos, sloths, and three species of monkeys. You can hike the trails on your own, with a guide (extra charge), or come back in the evening for a night tour. Be sure to bring ID to show when you pay the entrance fee.

MONTEVERDE CLOUD FOREST BIOLOGICAL RESERVE

From here, it's a 3km (1.5-mile) hike to the **Monteverde Cloud Forest Biological Reserve** ⓭ (tel: 2645-5122; www.reservamonteverde.com; daily 7am–4pm). This is the main reason to be here and the most popular, so visitors are limited to 250 at a time. Arrive as early as you can to get the

The suspension bridge makes a good lookout at Monteverde Cloud Forest Reserve

most out of the 13km (8 miles) of trails through a forest of giant prehistoric ferns and majestic trees weighed down with bromeliads and orchids. There's a thrilling suspension bridge to cross and a dramatic waterfall along the way. But the main quest here is a sighting of a resplendent quetzal.

On your first outing, it's a good idea to join a small, guided group (extra charge) for a natural history walk and take advantage of the guide's eyes and expertise. Then you can head out on the trails, with a map in hand, to explore on your own. Serious bird-watchers can sign up for a 4.5-hour guided tour (six people maximum, extra charge) in the hope of spotting some of the preserve's 500 or so bird species.

Always bring rain gear and wear waterproof hiking shoes. This is a cloud forest

and when it isn't raining, the mist is still cool and wet and the paths are muddy. A public bus back to Santa Elena leaves the preserve at 11.30am, 2pm, and 4pm. If you stay on or come back for the 5.45pm night tour, the tour fee includes transfer to and from the preserve.

HUMMINGBIRD GALLERY

Across from the entrance to the preserve, follow the steps up to the **Hummingbird Gallery** ⑭ (daily 10am–4.30pm; free, but donation expected), abuzz with dozens of hummingbirds darting between feeders and the surrounding bushes and trees. This is a photographer's paradise and the highlight of many visits to Monteverde.

The store here has an exhibition of the remarkable photos of Michael and Patricia Fogden, who spent two decades recording the fauna of Monteverde. You can buy a copy of their glossy *Hummingbirds of Costa Rica*, the definitive photographic study, along with other souvenirs.

SANTA ELENA CLOUD FOREST RESERVE

Some 5km (3 miles) northeast of Santa Elena, the **Santa Elena Cloud Forest Reserve** ⑮ (tel: 2645-5390; www.reservasantaelena.org; daily 7am–4pm) covers 310 hectares (765 acres) of misty forest, crisscrossed with 12km (7.5 miles) of nature trails. There are a variety of walking tours to choose from: from self-guided to private guided tours and group tours in

Monteverde Tour

If you'd like to learn about Monteverde's history and development, the Monteverde Footprints Tour, a two-hour commentated walk (tel: 2645-6565; www.exploremonteverde.com), gives the inside story, from the earliest Costa Rican gold-prospector settlers to the arrival of the Quakers and the development of conservation and nature preserves. The tour starts at 2pm at the Cheese Factory and ends at the Monteverde Café with a cup of coffee and insights into sustainable agriculture and coffee growing. All proceeds go to the non-profit Monteverde Community Fund.

Orchid Coffee Shop

English (at 7.30am, 9.15am, 11.30am and 1pm). It's smaller than Monteverde but also much less crowded. From a lookout tower, on clear days, you can see Arenal Volcano, along with many of the same bird and animal species you might see in Monteverde. The preserve is a non-profit project of the local high school and all funds raised go to maintaining the preserve and educational programs. Call 8725-4335 for a ride to the preserve from Santa Elena.

For a memorable cloud-forest adventure, overnight at the San Gerardo Station, a 4km- (2.5-mile) hike down from the Santa Elena Reserve. You can explore another 7km (4.5 miles) of trails around the lodge.

Food and Drink

① ORCHID COFFEE SHOP

150 meters/yds south of Banco Nacional, Santa Elena; tel: 2645-6850; $
More than a coffee shop – although there are 25 coffee drinks offered – the huge menu ranges from breakfast waffles and Eggs Benedict to veggie panini, and vegan tomato soup. It's artsy and lively, with free Wi-Fi.

② DE LUCIA

125 meters/yds west of Cerro Plano school; tel: 2645-5337; daily 11.30am–3pm and 4–9.30pm; $$
In this cheerful and colorful Chilean restaurant steaks and sea bass are grilled to perfection and smothered in garlic butter. Order a glass of Argentinian wine to accompany the complimentary tortillas with guacamole.

③ CELAJES

Hotel Belmar; www.hotelbelmar.net; daily 6.30–10am and noon–9pm; $$$
Celajes, or 'colored clouds,' is the most sophisticated dining in the area, with sunset views over the Gulf of Nicoya. Home-cooking here means innovative takes on Costa Rican dishes using farm-to-table ingredients from the hotel's organic garden. The menu is seasonal, but there's always a killer *tiramisú*.

④ CAFÉ CABURÉ RESTAURANT & CHOCOLATE SHOP

Next door to Bat Jungle, Monteverde; tel: 2645-5020; www.cabure.net; Mon–Sat 9am–9pm; $$.
Start with a chicken, beef, or vegetable empanada, then eat your way around the world at this chic restaurant, with curry, satay, and *mole* flavors spicing up wraps, salads, and mains. Save room for Death by Brownie and at least one truffle from the chocolate store.

⑤ TRAMONTI PIZZERIA E RISTORANTE

El Bosque Lodge, across from Bat Jungle; tel: 2645-6120; www.tramonticr.com; daily 11.30am–9.45pm; $$
The most popular Italian restaurant in the area. Choose from wood-fired pizzas and calzones, homemade pastas, and meats and fish, including a hearty sausage and polenta plate. Come early for a table on busy weekends, or better still, make a reservation.

SOUTHERN NICOYA PENINSULA

The idyllic tropical beach vacation of travel brochures is alive and well and living along the southwest coast of the Nicoya Peninsula. The far-stretching pristine beaches are perfect for surfing, strolling, and staring into sunsets, far from crowds or high-rise, resort hotels.

DISTANCE: 100km (62 miles)
START: Town of Nicoya
END: Punta Islita
POINTS TO NOTE: SANSA and NATUREAIR planes fly from San José to Nosara if you prefer to arrive quickly and rent a car. There is a shorter, very rough beach road between Nosara and Sámara, starting east of Garza, but it can only be driven in dry season, January through April; a 4x4 vehicle is recommended. From Punta Islita, you can return to the mainland by driving north along a paved highway to Carmonal, then continuing north toward Mansion and the road to the Friendship Bridge. Or you can head east from Carmonal to Lepanto and take the Naranjo car ferry across the Gulf of Nicoya to Puntarenas and the mainland. Check the Coonatramar ferry schedule at www.coonatramar.com, tel: 2661-2084. A car with two passengers costs about $20.

ters. While the northwestern beaches are well developed, with high-rise resort hotels catering to sun-seeking 'snow-birds' on package tours, the once-remote southern stretch of coast, from Nosara to Punta Islita, has happily escaped such intense tourist development.

No longer remote thanks to improved roads and a bridge connecting the peninsula to the mainland, these beach communities attract independent travelers to mostly small-scale lodges and beach hotels, large-scale surf breaks, cosmopolitan restaurants, outdoor adventures, and nature preserves.

Nosara has more of a laid-back, sophisticated, new-age vibe, while Sámara has more of a casual, fun, and family feeling. But both communities have stretches of pristine beach where you really can get away from it all.

NICOYA

Whether you arrive via the road from the Friendship Bridge over the Tempisque River, or take the car ferry from Puntarenas to Naranjo (an adventure in

The Nicoya Peninsula's Pacific coastline stretches for hundreds of kilome-

Glorious, palm-fringed Playa Sámara

itself), all roads lead to **Nicoya**. The only reminder of this town's colonial heyday as a provincial capital is the handsome, white-adobe **Church of San Blas ❶**, at the north side of the central park.

Modern Nicoya is a bustling commercial center, with supermarkets, banks, pharmacies, and 24-hour gas stations. It's a good idea to stock up on anything you need here before heading south.

Drive south out of town on Route 150, following signs for Nosara and Sámara. The road is paved, with occasional potholes, and plenty of ups and downs and river crossings. The scenery is bucolic,

with large tracts of cattle pasture backed by wooded hills and rows of tall palms. You'll drive through small, neat communities centered on the traditional Tico trio of soccer field, school, and church.

NOSARA

At the 28km (17-mile) mark, watch for the gas station on the left; about a kilometer (0.6 mile) south of the station, take the turn signed Nosara. The road is a little rough, but at least there are now bridges over the rivers. After 8km (5 miles) you will join up with the beach

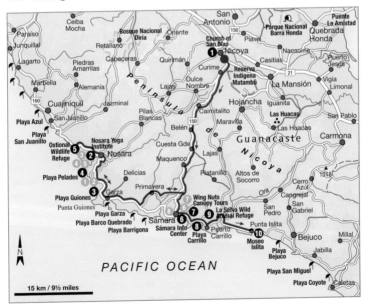

Catching up in Nicoya town

road, Route 160, at **Garza**, a small fishing village. Now the road does get bumpy – and dusty or muddy, depending on the season – for the next 10km (6 miles).

Just before you enter town, you'll pass the **Nosara Yoga Institute ❷** (tel: 2682-0071; 8.30am–5.30pm), which offers a variety of yoga classes set in a peaceful, tropical garden.

A few minutes more brings you to the intersection with the road to Playa Guiones. Look for the Café de Paris on the corner and turn left. This road is lined with stores selling beachwear, yoga gear, the latest surfing equipment, local crafts, and souvenirs. Just past the bank (and ATM), **Robin's Café & Ice Cream** (see ❶) is worth a stop to enjoy her homemade ice cream and exotic vegetarian fare.

Almost at the end of the road is the entrance, on the right, to the **Harmony Hotel** (see page 115), the most luxuriously green hotel in town, with a holistic spa, a garden juice bar, and the town's top **restaurant** (see ❷).

PLAYA GUIONES

About 300 meters/yds on, you reach **Playa Guiones ❸**, a 7km (4.5-mile) stretch of beige sand, perfect for jogging, cycling, practicing yoga poses at sunrise and sunset, surfing or just sitting and watching the surfers ride the waves. The thing that makes this beach so special is the lack of development. You will see only waves crashing on the shore and wide swaths of sand edged by tendrils of sea grape vines, bordered by shade trees screening from view a few low-lying hotels.

PLAYA PELADES

Back up on the main road, continue west to the third exit on the left, signed for **El Chivo** (see ❸), a Mexican *cantina* where every day is a fiesta, and **Il Peperoni** (see ❹), an alfresco, brick-oven pizzeria. The road ends at crescent-shaped **Playa Pelades ❹**, where the surf is a little calmer and the beach is dotted with fishing boats. Locals and visitors gather late each afternoon to watch the sunset and the passing parade of people. The best vantage point is from **La Luna Bar & Grill** (see ❺), overlooking the beach, lounging on an Indonesian couch and sipping a tropical cocktail.

RÍO NOSARA

Back on the main road, continue west and take the uphill road on the left, signed for **Lagarta Lodge** (see page 115), a very comfortable eco-lodge, high on a hill with a bird's-eye view of the **Río Nosara** emptying into the ocean. The lodge has a private nature preserve bordering the river, where serious bird-watchers can sign up for an early-morning tour with **Experience Nosara** guides (tel: 8705-2010; www. experience-nosara.com).

Another way to explore the river and its avian and crocodilian denizens is on

Plenty of space at Playa Guiones

a River Safari (tel: 2682-0610), floating on a flat-bottomed boat with an expert naturalist guide.

OSTIONAL NATIONAL WILDLIFE REFUGE

Drive another 7km (4.5 miles) north of Nosara, following the main coastal road, to the **Ostional National Wildlfe Refuge ⑤**, which protects the *arribadas* (mass nestings) of olive ridley turtles. Turtles can number in the thousands over the course of several nights, usually before a new moon. Visitors must reserve ahead to join a guide-led tour organized by a village cooperative (tel: 2682-0428).

PLAYA SÁMARA

From Nosara, retrace the route along Route 160 to the turnoff from Route 150, but this time, follow Route 150 south, into the center of Sámara. Drive down the main street, past the bougainvillea-covered **Hotel Giada** (see page 116) and turn left onto the sandy road along the beach. Park wherever you can and get out and walk.

For your first look at the beach, you can't do better than taking a table at beachfront **Gusto Creativo Italiano** (see ⑥), the coolest restaurant in town, literally, with breezes off the ocean. With your feet already in the sand, you can gaze out at Isla Chora, at the south end of the beach and watch the waves break over the reef that keeps the water calm for swimming and kayaking.

Next door is the invaluable **Sámara InfoCenter ⑥** (tel: 2656-2424; www.samarainfocenter.com), beside the Lo Que Hay Bar y Taquería, where you can get breakfast as early as 7am and a taco as late as midnight. Stop in for detailed maps of the town listing all the restaurants and hotels, and knowledgeable advice in English.

If you return here in the evening, cross the street from the InfoCenter to check out the tiny, retro Micro Bar, which opens its doors after 4pm, spilling out onto the street. For $1, try a sample of any of the 24 craft beers on tap.

Unlike Nosara, Sámara's beachfront has small terrace restaurants and beach bars, pyramids of surfboards advertising surf schools, and kayaks ready to rent and paddle. **La Vela Latina Beach Bar** (see ⑦) has tables on a terrace and on the beach, which tend to fill up at sunset.

Fans of gourmet cuisine should not leave Sámara without dining at **Mama Guí** (see ⑧) an improbably sophisticated outpost of contemporary Italian cuisine with tropical accents, a little off the beaten beach path. Book ahead to be sure of a table at this chic restaurant, where Gigio Palazzo, a celebrated chef from Puglia, via New York City, holds court, emerging often from the kitchen to describe his latest delectable creations.

Within a five-minute walk heading east, you'll find yourself pretty much alone on

Flawless Playa Carrillo

the wide beach. The 5km (3-mile) beach ends at a forested outcropping, in front of **Villas Playa Sámara** (see page 116), a family-friendly collection of villas set in a mature tropical garden, steps from the beach. Walking west takes you past a few beach bars and restaurants with tables on the sand, shaded by beach almond and palm trees.

Retracing your steps to your car, get back up to Route 150, and turn right toward Playa Carrillo, 5km (3 miles) east. You'll pass by the office of **Wing Nuts Canopy Tour** ❼ (tel: 2656-0153; www.wingnutscanopy.com), where you can book a three-hour zip-line tour through the jungle, with ocean views. This outfit takes particularly good care of children and anxious first-timers.

The road climbs steeply after the entrance to Villas Playa Sámara, then flattens out as you approach **Playa Carrillo** ❽. Often cited as the most picturesque spot in Costa Rica, it's a perfect crescent beach, backed by coconut palms. It can be busy with picnickers on weekends, but on weekdays you may have it all to yourself.

LA SELVA WILD ANIMAL REFUGE

Local lore has it that the rivers that empty into Playa Carrillo at each end of the beach are home to crocodiles. True or not, these bathing spots are usually avoided.

To see a crocodile in a safe situation, visit **La Selva Wild Animal Refuge** ❾

(tel: 2656-2236; daily 8.30am–7pm). Make a left at the south end of the beach and follow the signs uphill on a dirt road. Run by Italian animal lovers, this slightly ramshackle rescue center houses crocodiles and caimans, snakes, tortoises, wild cats, and hard-to-see nocturnal creatures. You can visit early in the day and come back in the evening to catch nocturnal animals active. Be sure to wear closed shoes with socks since biting ants may make an appearance.

PUNTA ISLITA

Heading east, the road climbs up from the beach, then dips down to cross the Río Ora over a narrow bridge. From here it's a scenic, hilly drive to **Punta Islita**, 16km (10 miles) southeast of Carrillo.

Famous for the five-star Punta Islita Hotel (see page 116), with its private landing strip and ultra-luxurious suites and villas, the other main attraction here is the **Museo Islita** ❿ (tel: 2656-2039; Mon–Sat 8.30am–noon and 1–4.30pm), an open-air contemporary art museum, where the entire village has become the art. Trees, houses, school, church – every building is covered with murals, painted or mosaic, all created by locals and visiting resident artists. At the visitors' center you can buy a colorful map that details all the art around the village, browse the art gallery, and purchase small art works.

Fresh flavors and airy setting at Harmony restaurant

Food and Drink

① ROBIN'S CAFÉ & ICE CREAM
Road to Playa Guiones; tel: 2682-0617; daily 8.30am–4.30pm; $
In addition to the homemade ice-cream and freshly-baked brownies, Robin serves breakfast all day and healthy, tasty Asian-flavored vegetarian and raw-food plates.

② HARMONY HOTEL RESTAURANT
Road to Playa Guiones; tel: 2682-4114; www. harmonynosara.com; daily breakfast 7am–10am, lunch noon–3pm, dinner 6–9pm; $$$$
This chic, retro dining terrace uses ingredients from the hotel's organic garden. Light dishes include a smoked mushroom salad, coconut fish soup, or a veggie green curry. Fresh fish and scampi top the mains menu. Save room for passion fruit cheesecake. There's also an outdoor sushi lounge and garden juice bar.

③ EL CHIVO
Road to Playa Pelada; tel: 2682-0887; www. elchivo.co; Mon–Sat 11am–10pm, Sun 9am–10pm; $$
Come for traditional Mexican favorites with contemporary flavors, pitchers of sangria, and Mexican beers on tap at the cantina bar, along with tequila cocktails. The atmosphere is festive, day and night.

④ IL PEPERONI
Road to Playa Pelada, across from Condominios Las Flores; tel: 2682-0545; daily 11am–10pm; $$
Choose from thin-crust pizza with myriad toppings and baked in a brick oven, pasta, Italian-style seafood, or grilled meat.

⑤ LA LUNA BAR & GRILL
Overlooking Playa Pelada; tel: 2682-0122; daily 7am–11pm; $$
Mediterranean flavors rule at this beach restaurant. Start with spicy hummus and pitas, Moroccan-style grilled fish as a main, and Nutella and banana pizza for dessert. At breakfast, it's *típico* or American-style.

⑥ GUSTO CREATIVO ITALIANO
Beachfront, 50 meters/yds off the main street; tel: 2656-0252; $$
Sámara's hippest, liveliest beach club, with tables on the sand, also serves great Italian fare all day. Toast the sunset with a glass of Prosecco.

⑦ LA VELA LATINA BEACH BAR
On beach road, across from Villas Kalimba; tel: 2656-2286; daily noon–midnight; $$
A slightly older crowd gathers to this terrace bar with leather-and-wood chairs and soft salsa and jazz music. Sushi rolls and Asian noodles keep hunger at bay.

⑧ MAMA GUÍ
West of Catholic Church; tel: 2656-2347; 5–11pm; $$$ (cash only)
Feast on innovative, contemporary Italian dishes with a tropical twist Start with tuna carpaccio dressed with passion fruit and lemon zest. Homemade pastas are delicate and even the salads here are a revelation.

Heron at Braulio Carrillo National Park

CARIBBEAN COAST

Think Caribbean and most visitors picture turquoise water, palm-lined beaches, sunny skies – and luxury resorts. This Caribbean coast has all the above, but, except for a few upscale boutique hotels, the atmosphere here is lively, young, casual, and definitely not fancy.

DISTANCE: 74km (46 miles)

TIME: Two days driving, walking, and cycling.

START: Puerto Limón

END: Manzanillo

POINTS TO NOTE: You do need a car to drive the whole route. But you can park your car wherever you are lodging and cover a lot of the ground, from Puerto Viejo to Manzanillo, on a bicycle. Be aware that there are often powerful undertows and dangerous currents on most of the beaches. Theft and petty crime are common, and there is a fair amount of drug trafficking and usage. It's best to avoid the rowdy late-night bars, especially in Puerto Viejo. At night, take taxis to your hotel and avoid deserted beaches. As ever, don't leave belongings or valuables unattended on the beach or in a car.

A couple of centuries ago, this coastal area was settled by English-speaking Afro-Caribbean fishermen and their families, joining the indigenous groups that settled much earlier in the mountains higher up, fleeing the Spanish conquistadors. It wasn't until Highway 32 was finished in the 1980s, connecting the central valley to the coast, that tourism blossomed and brought visitors from Europe, Canada, and the US.

Today, this coast attracts a mix of young surfers, foreign-language students, nature-lovers, party-goers, and sun worshippers, all drawn to the low-key, carefree, relaxed vibe and the coast's natural beauty. There's still a sense of feeling remote from the rest of the world here. And that may be the greatest attraction of all.

GETTING THERE

Whether by bus or car, the drive to Costa Rica's Caribbean Coast is an adventure in itself. The first 64km (40 miles) of the highway pass through the vast wilderness of **Braulio Carrillo National Park**, 475 sq km (183 sq miles) of primary rain forest and cloud forest. Work on the road started in 1967, to replace the earthquake-damaged railroad that

Cuties at the Sloth Sanctuary

Riding the waves at Playa Grande

once connected the central valley to the Caribbean coast, and it took more than 20 years to build.

The Caribbean Coast officially starts in the port city of Limón. But most visitors want to experience pristine beaches, not a slightly run-down, truck-congested port. To get your Caribbean visit off to a more pleasant start, you can bypass Limón by turning right off Route 32 onto Route 241 south, signed for Santa Rosa. Look for the turnoff between the Del Monte container yard and the stoplight in Liverpool.

After the narrow bridge over the Río Vizcaya, you get your first glimpse of beach and coconut palms, along with the first whiff of the briny Atlantic Ocean. You'll pass roadside stands selling coconut oil, harvested from those palms. Just over the Río Banano bridge, Route 241 merges into Route 36, heading south along the coast to Puerto Viejo.

SLOTH SANCTUARY

About 20km (12.5 miles) along Route 36, you'll see large sloth-crossing signs indicating the **Sloth Sanctuary of Costa Rica** ❶ (www.slothsanctuary.com; Tue–Sun 8am–2pm), the country's first rescue center for these endearing creatures. The two-hour tour takes in the sloth nursery and a photo op with Buttercup, the first rescued sloth, now 25 years old, holding court in her hanging basket. You can shop for rather expensive but cute plush-toy sloths in every size and color – including neon pink – or even sloth-themed socks.

PLAYA GRANDE

Continuing south, bear left at Penshurst gas station, heading to Cahuita. Just after the *puesto de control* (customs police station) take the rough dirt and stone road on the left, signed for **Magellan Boutique Hotel** (see page 117), a very small, very romantic hotel in a garden near Playa Grande.

At the T-junction, turn left to reach **Tree of Life** ❷ (tel: 8317-0325; www.treeoflifecostarica.com; Tue–Sun, guided tour at 11am only, July–Aug and Nov–Mar) another wildlife rescue center. (The area's animals do seem to need a lot of rescuing.) Among the animals you'll see during the 1.5h tour are sloths, monkeys, kinkajous, raccoons, and iguanas. This refuge also has a 4-hectare (10-acre) botanical garden, visited as part of the tour.

PLAYA NEGRA

Reverse direction and head south, following the beach road skirting **Playa Negra** ❸, a very shallow beach with dark sand and usually warm swimmable water, although it's often littered with driftwood. On moonlit nights it's a favorite of discrete skinny dippers.

Scattered along the beach road are small hotels and casual cafés, including Brigitte's, a breakfast favorite, where

Blue land crab in Cahuita National Park

you can also rent bicycles, the preferred form of transportation here. You can't miss the huge toucan sculpture advertising beachfront **Atlantida Lodge** (see page 116), hidden in the jungle. During the day there's a breezy beachfront bar. If you're looking for a party after sunset, the huge, outdoor Kukula Bar serves pizzas and shakes up some good cocktails.

Just past the soccer field, **Sobra Las Olas** (see ❶) overlooking the beach, focuses more seriously on cooking fish and seafood. It's relaxing at lunch and romantic at dinner, with the sound of waves breaking on the shore. Nearby is lovely **El Encanto Hotel and Spa** (see page 116), set in a lush garden, far enough out of town to be an oasis of calm but close enough to walk to Cahuita's lively main street.

MISS EDITH

The dirt road becomes a residential street, and about 10 minutes' walk brings you to one of the main reasons to visit Cahuita: the institution that is **Miss Edith** (see ❷), a bastion of old-style, spicy Afro-Caribbean cuisine in a breezy, open-air dining room.

On one side of Miss Edith's is Cahuita Inn Pizzeria, all chic, sleek, and Italian, serving authentic pizza. On the other side, right on the shoreline and surrounded by boats, is The Snorkeling House (tel: 8361-1924), the place to book a snorkeling trip to the nearby reef or other ocean adventures.

CAHUITA NATIONAL PARK

Next door is the brand new **Cahuita National Park Office** ❹ (daily 8am–4pm) with a breezy, seafront promenade and benches, restrooms, and cold outdoor showers. There's no set admission fee at this entrance to the park, but visitors are encouraged to make a donation of at least $5 each.

The park stretches for 3km (2 miles) along Playa Blanca, a picturesque, white-sand beach backed by rain forest. A nature trail runs through the forest, and there's a camping area at the Puerto Vargas entrance, 5km (3 miles) farther south, where you pay $5. Be prepared to fend off raccoons and coatis looking for a free meal. The offshore coral reef protected by the national park was badly damaged by an earthquake, so snorkeling is only permitted with a certified guide.

CAHUITA TOWN

A right turn (west) from Miss Edith's takes you into **Cahuita** ❺ proper, a small, slightly scruffy town, with a few faded Caribbean-style houses sporting painted gingerbread trim. Tourism is the main business, as you'll see along the town's colorful but short main drag, home to a jumble of souvenir shops, small supermarkets, and casual restaurants.

Two dueling bars face off across a street corner: Coco's Bar, a sometimes raucous, reggae-loud local, and Ricky's

Cahuita street scene

Bar, a slightly more relaxed place to enjoy a quiet drink and watch the parade of young, scantily clad, beach-loving tourists, mostly from Europe, Canada, and the US.

BOTANICAL GARDEN

Heading toward Puerto Viejo, 16km (10 miles) south on Route 36, running parallel to the beach, don't expect to see the spruced-up charm of developed Caribbean island resorts. You'll pass houses of widely varying styles and standards, yet there's something about the Caribbean setting amid coconut trees that gives even a ramshackle house a picturesque quality.

Just before you cross the bridge into Puerto Viejo, look for a sign on the right to **Finca La Isla Botanical Garden ❻** (tel: 8886-8530; Fri–Mon 10am–4pm). There's prime bird-watching along the road leading to the garden as well as in the garden, which has mature fruit and spice trees. It's also a working organic farm,

and garden tours include fruit and chocolate tastings.

Playa Puerto Viejo

PUERTO VIEJO DE TALAMANCA

While Cahuita has a certain shabby dignity, **Puerto Viejo de Talamanca** ❼ (to distinguish it from Puerto Viejo de Sarapiquí, farther north) is not pretty. At the entrance to town there's an abandoned rusted-out barge that has been 'gracing' the otherwise attractive black-sand beach for decades. The main street is a hodgepodge of souvenir shops, unattractive commercial buildings, dilapidated wooden houses, and cars parked higgledy-piggledy. Basically this is a busy tourist town, a favorite of surfers and young backpackers, as well as a few unsavory local characters you want to avoid.

That said many dilapidated houses are being renovated and turned into trendy stores, bars, and restaurants. Off the main drag, on the west side of town, there are some lovely old houses in a residential section with gardens. If you want to stay close to the action in town,

> ### Danger, Danger
>
> It's a spectacular drive, but also a dangerous one, especially in rain or fog, both of which are frequent, as are landslides. Give yourself plenty of time and drive slowly and cautiously. You will be sharing the road with huge transportation and tanker trucks, ferrying cargo between the Central Valley and Puerto Limón. Count on at least four hours to drive from San José to Limón.

the most pleasant option is **Casa Verde Lodge** (see page 117).

Playa Puerto Viejo

The public beach stretches the entire length of town. Offshore, at the southern end is the **Salsa Brava**, a challenging surfers' break. Along the beachfront dirt road, a few ramshackle buildings survive, including the town's original general store. The tables in front of **Johnny's Bar** are close enough to the water to get your feet wet. At the end of the road, on the corner, Pan Pay (see ❾) is a perfectly located early-morning bakery/restaurant. Order coffee and a huge chocolate croissant, grab a table to catch the ocean breeze, and watch the surfers at play.

Chocolate paradise

One of the best reasons to visit town is chocolate, once an economic mainstay before a fungus wiped out the cacao plantations. Happily, cacao is making a comeback. As evidenced at **Bread and Chocolate** (see ❹), across from the Interbus office, where they make five varieties of fudgy brownies, half a dozen chocolate-cake varieties, and handmade truffles.

A block south, on Calle 217, chic, minimalist **CHO.CO Boutique** ❽ (tel: 6363-4274; www.cho.co.cr; 11am–8pm), showcases locally sourced chocolate. Browse the wall displays of each plantation's chocolate bars or indulge in a taste pairing of chocolates with wines, craft beers, or local rums. The boutique

Boards at the ready on Playa Cocles

also organizes tours to nearby chocolate farms.

Luluberlu Gallery

Around the corner from Bread and Chocolate, on Avenida 69, between Calle 215 and 217, **LuluBerlu Local Artist Gallery** ❾ (tel: 2750-0394; daily 9am–9pm), is a tile-and-glass-fronted emporium of exceptional local art, where you'll be tempted at every corner by exquisite jewelry, mosaic tiles, whimsical children's dolls and backpacks, sophisticated seashell and paper lampshades, and chic beachwear.

Caribbean flavors

Restaurant Tamara (see ❺), on the main street at the corner of Calle 217, has been serving traditional, home-style Caribbean fare since 1983. You can't go wrong with the chicken in spicy Caribbean sauce, with coconut rice and red beans.

For a lighter snack to take on a beach picnic, check out the homemade, spicy chicken, beef, or vegetable patties for sale from stands along Main Street and up Calle 217. Sweets include banana cake and *pan bon*, Caribbean-style gingerbread. Wash it down with a glass of lime and ginger juice.

If you're interested in indigenous culture and nature tours, drop into the **Talamanca Association for Ecotourism and Conservation (ATEC)** ❿ (tel: 2750-0398; www.ateccr.org) on Main Street. This nonprofit group organizes cultural tours, with visits to indigenous villages and activities from Caribbean cooking classes to weaving thatch roofs. ATEC also organizes nature, hiking, bird-watching, and horseback tours with local guides.

PLAYA COCLES

Driving south from Puerto Viejo – by car or, better still, by bicycle – along the paved road, you'll pass an almost continuous string of restaurants and bars, lodges, and B&Bs, ranging from backpacker-basic hostels to ultra-luxe, small resorts. About 2km (1.2 miles) south of Puerto Viejo is **Playa Cocles** ⓫, a pleasant, light-sanded beach that is a little less busy than the town beach.

PLAYA CHIQUITA

Another 4km (2 miles) south, the road passes **Playa Chiquita** ⓬, where you may even have the beach to yourself at sunrise. If your lodging isn't close to a beach, you can hang out at the high-style **Noa Beach Club**, with pink hammocks, padded loungers, a bar, and an upscale restaurant –all part of the stylish **Le Caméléon Hotel** across the road (but the beach club is open to non-guests). Nearby is the more affordable but no less charming **Physis Caribbean B&B** (see page 117).

South of the soccer field, follow the smell of baking bread to **Panadería Frances** (tel: 8498-3901; 6am–7pm), where the French baker makes his own version of a *pain au chocolat* – bread rolls,

not pastry, oozing rich, creamy chocolate. Across the street is dinner-only **Pecora Nera** (see page 123), the Caribbean's first, and still finest, Italian restaurant.

PLAYA PUNTA UVA

Another 3km (2 miles) farther south lies **Playa Punta Uva** ⓭, the most beautiful and the least crowded beach on the coast, with crystalline, aquamarine water and the best snorkeling just meters off shore. The long, curved beach also has the distinction of facing west, so it's the only shoreline location where you can catch spectacular sunsets.

The sandy road along the beach has tree-shaded nooks where you can park and set up your beach towel. There's just one open-air, casual restaurant on the beach, **Arrecife** (daily 7am–7pm), where you can order fresh fish or Caribbean chicken and take advantage of the restrooms.

En route to Punta Uva, just past the *liceo* (school), keep an eye out on the right for the glowing globes hanging in front of **Maya Shanti Natural Art** ⓮ (daily 9am–4pm). This is the showroom of a Swiss expat artist who incorporates dried flowers and leaves into lustrous papier-mâché lampshades.

ARA PROJECT

Continuing south on Route 256, watch on the right side of the road for a wooden sign with a green macaw and the name

Ara Project ⓯ (tel: 8971-1436; www. thearaproject.org; daily 4pm guided tour by reservation only). Bird-watchers and photographers eager to see one of these rare, colorful macaws, currently on the endangered species list, will want to visit this reintroduction station.

PLAYA MANZANILLO

You have almost reached the end of the road – some 15km (9 miles) from Puerto Viejo – when you reach **Manzanillo** ⓰, a small fishing village with a long, palm-shaded beach and calm, swimming waters protected by a reef. It's blissfully quiet here except on Sundays, when day-trippers from Limón often arrive by the busload.

The main action is at **Restaurante Maxi's** (see ④), which has a bar/disco downstairs and a breezy restaurant upstairs, overlooking the beach.

For people who like the idea of camping but don't want to rough it, **Almonds & Corals Hotel** (see page 117), in the middle of the jungle just before you reach Manzanillo, has very comfortable safari tents on high platforms, complete with electricity and bathrooms.

GANDOCA-MANZANILLO WILDLIFE REFUGE

A short walk south along the beach takes you into the wild heart of the **Refugio Nacional de Vida Silvestre Gandoca-Manzanillo** ⓱ (daily 8am–4pm; free). This huge preserve protects swamplands,

Refugio Nacional de Vida Silvestre Gandoca-Manzanillo

coral reefs, turtle-nesting grounds, and the only mangrove forest on Costa Rica's Caribbean coast. Hiking trails climb up into forest where birds and wildlife abound. It takes three to four hours to reach Punta Mona and you can arrange to be picked up by boat there. To get the most out of a hike – and to avoid getting lost –contact local guide Florentino Drenald (tel: 8841-2732), or ATEC in Puerto Viejo.

Food and Drink

① SOBRA LAS OLAS
Beach road south of the soccer field, Cahuita; tel: 2755-0109; Wed–Mon noon–10pm; $$
Red snapper is the house specialty at this upscale seafood and pasta restaurant, perched over the waves. The ocean view is the main decor but it's enough.

② MISS EDITH
75 meters/yds north of Cahuita National Park office, Cahuita; tel: 2755-0248; Thu–Tue noon–9.30pm; $$
The original Miss Edith is no more, but her daughter has taken over this humble temple paying homage to Afro-Caribbean home cooking, from curried rice to jerk chicken to *rondón*, a spicy stew of tender root vegetables and seafood or chicken. No credit cards.

③ PAN PAY
South end of Beach Road, Puerto Viejo; tel: 2750-0081; daily 7am–4pm; $
The aroma of strong coffee and croissants will draw you in for an early breakfast. A thick slice of the hefty Spanish omelet is a lunch in itself. Tables with a breezy beach view are perfect for people watching. No credit cards.

④ BREAD AND CHOCOLATE
Across from Interbus office, Calle 215; tel: 2750-0723; Tue–Sat 6.30am–6.30pm, Sun 6.30am–2.30pm; $
Along with the delectable brownies, muffins, and chocolate cakes – including a fudgy Queen of Sheba and a vegan version – there are also savory dishes: standouts include biscuits smothered in mushroom gravy, and sautéed potatoes topped with Jerk BBQ sauce. No cards.

⑤ RESTAURANT TAMARA
Main Street, 25 meters/yds north of Calle 217; tel: 2750-0148; daily 11.30am–10pm; $
Come for a taste of authentic Caribbean cooking at this pleasant, open-air restaurant. For a light lunch, there's shrimp salad. For a real splurge, order lobster for two with salad, fried plantains, and rice and beans.

⑥ RESTAURANTE MAXI'S
Manzanillo beach; tel: 2759-9073; daily noon–9pm; $$
Fish and seafood couldn't be any fresher than at this cheerful restaurant, served on huge platters with salad, grilled vegetables, and *patacones*. Rice and beans here have a different accent, using Panamanian *guandú* beans. The downstairs bar vibrates at night with recorded reggae.

DIRECTORY

Hand-picked hotels and restaurants to suit all budgets and tastes, organized by area, plus select nightlife listings, an alphabetical listing of practical information, a language guide, and an overview of the best books and films to give you a flavor of the country.

Hotel Don Carlos

ACCOMMODATIONS

Costa Rica is no longer quite the bargain it once was. The national standard of living has risen considerably in the last 10 years, along with travelers' expectations of modern comforts and electronic connectivity.

There's still a wide range of affordable accommodations, from delightful B&Bs, rustic but comfortable cabinas, to small, friendly family-run hotels and eco-lodges. Some of the most expensive lodgings are in the most remote areas, since it's costly to transport food and supplies and to house live-in staff. Most remote eco-lodges list all-inclusive rates that may seem high, but usually include all meals, resident guides, tours, and activities.

Christmas and New Year's, along with the week before Easter, are the busiest times for lodgings, especially along the coasts. Book early if you're visiting at those times. High season is typically mid-December to April when the climate is sunniest and driest. 'Green season,' from April to November, offers lower prices when the rains come.

> Prices are for a double room in regular high season, breakfast and tax included.
> $$$$=over $250
> $$$= $150–$250
> $$= $100–$150
> $ = $50–$100

Most hotels and lodges include breakfast, either a light Continental or a hearty, full desayuno. When breakfast is not included, it's noted in the review. When booking, make sure the hotel prices quoted include the 16.4 percent government tax.

San José

Hotel Don Carlos

Barrio Amón, Calle 9 Avenida 9; tel: 2221-6707; www.doncarloshotel.com; $
This historical hotel has peaceful interior courtyards, art-lined corridors, a pleasant terrace restaurant, and one of the city's best gift shops. The excellent-value rooms are spacious, with traditional furnishings, and there's free parking.

Hotel Grano de Oro

Calle 30, Avenida 2–4; tel: 2255-3322; www.hotelgranodeoro; $$$
This elegant hotel merges two historical houses with an elegant Victorian-style addition that's home to downtown's best restaurant (see page 118). Blending antiques and contemporary touches, all the rooms are spacious and elegant. The less expensive rooms are in the original wing, looking onto a garden.

Posada del Museo

Avenida 2, Calle 7; tel: 2258-1027; www.hotelposadadelmuseo.com; $

A room at Orosí Lodge

The central pond at Trogón Lodge

Cozy, colonial-style rooms fill this Victorian house, set on a palm-lined pedestrian walkway. The pleasant first-floor café serves Argentine specialties. There's occasional train noise during the day.

Heredia

Hotel Bougainvillea

Santo Domingo de Heredia; tel: 2244-1414; www.hb.co.cr; $$

This 82-room, two-story hotel sits in a gorgeous garden of bougainvillea and orchids – a favorite with bird-watchers. Spacious rooms come with window screens so you can enjoy mountain air. Heated pool.

Orosí

Orosí Lodge

Three blocks east of soccer field, Orosí; tel: 2533-3578; www.orosilodge.com; $

This small chalet-style hotel has a pretty interior garden, and the charming rooms on the second floor have mountain and valley views. It's right in the middle of town, beside the thermal pools and within easy driving distance of Tapantí National Park.

Cerro de la Muerte

Dantica Lodge and Gallery

4km (2.5 miles) west of Inter-American Highway exit at Km 80; tel: 2740-1067; www.dantica.com; $$

The area's most sophisticated lodge has luxurious private bungalows with modern, European furnishings and Jacuzzis. Picture windows look out onto mountains and forest with hiking trails.

The Latin American artisan gallery showcases fine handicrafts.

Paraíso Quetzal Lodge

Km 70, Inter-American Highway; tel: 2299-0241; www.quetzalsparadise.com; $$

Frequent quetzal sightings and an active hummingbird gallery draw birders to this high-altitude, rustic lodge with private cabins with mountain views. Hot showers and heaters keep you warm at night. Guided hiking trails available.

Savegre Hotel, Natural Reserve & Spa

San Gerardo de Dota, 9km (5.5 miles) east of Inter-American Highway; tel: 2740-1028; www.savegre.com; $$

This bird-watcher's mecca has comfortable rooms in rustic cabins arranged around gardens planted to attract birds. Some suites have fireplaces and bathtubs. Resident guides lead tours over extensive hiking trails. The riverside spa offers comfort to sore feet and strained necks. Meals are usually buffet-style, featuring fresh trout.

Trogón Lodge

San Gerardo de Dota, 7km (4.5 miles) off Inter-American Highway; tel: 2293-8181; www.trogonlodge.com; $$

Duplex, wood cabins are arranged around a pond in a magical, flower-filled garden beside the rushing Savegre River. Each cabin has two double beds. Hiking forest trails and a zipline nearby.

South Pacific

Hotel Cristal Ballena

7km (4.5 miles) south of Uvita; tel: 2786-5354; www.cristal-ballena.com; $$$

Luxury with an ocean view and a large, scenic swimming pool are the attractions here. Suites are fully air-conditioned, with private terraces. Dine poolside by candlelight or enjoy fresh breezes at the buffet breakfast. The landscaped gardens have a fitness trail.

Hacienda Barú

2km (1.2 miles) north of Dominical; tel: 2787-0003; www.haciendabaru.com; $

Nature lovers flock to this eco-lodge and nature preserve with trails through primary and secondary forest, on the edge of a turtle-nesting beach. Resident guides lead birding and wildlife tours. Treetop adventures include a canopy tour. Two-bedroom cabins are perfect for families; spacious rooms facing a swimming pool are cool, comfortable, and affordable.

Kurá Design Villas

High above Uvita; tel: 8448-5744; www.kuracostarica.com; $$$$

This exclusive couples retreat is the height of luxury, as well as being high atop a hill. With stylish, contemporary furnishings, private terraces, glass showers for two with an ocean view, a spa, and candlelit dining by an infinity pool, there's no need to leave this cocoon.

Río Tico Safari Lodge

Vergel de Punta Mala, off the Costanera, 3km (2 miles) south of Ojochal; tel: 8996-7935; www.riotico.com; $

Comfortable safari tents pitched on platforms cantilevered over a rushing river come with all mod cons. You can ride horses and explore forest trails. Great for kids and the young at heart who are fit enough to climb some steps between river and road. Breakfast is extra.

Roca Verde

1km (0.6 miles) south of Dominical, off Costanera; tel: 2787-0036; www.rocaverde. net; $$

This small hotel is closest to the beach, so it's popular with surfers, anglers, and beachcombers. Rooms are modest but comfortable, facing a small pool. The open-air restaurant has great pizza and seafood, and there is a live bluesy-rock band on Friday nights.

Villas Río Mar

1km (0.6 miles) upriver from Dominical; tel: 2787-0052; www.villasriomar.com; $$

This affordable, riverside resort has tennis courts, a huge pool, an excellent restaurant, and gorgeous gardens. All bungalows have air-conditioning and terraces. The breakfast buffet is top notch.

Drake Bay

Casa Corcovado Jungle Lodge

North end of Corcovado National Park, by boat; tel: 2256-3181; www.casacorcovado. com; $$$$ (all-inclusive)

Luxurious bungalows at this eco-lodge on the doorstep of Corcovado come with

first-class food, naturalist guides, two pools, and a beach. Activities include snorkeling trips to Caño Island. The thrilling boat ride to get here is an adventure in itself. Minimum two-night stay.

Drake Bay Wilderness Resort

Drake Bay; tel: 2775-1715; www.drakebay. com; $$$ (all-inclusive)

This attractively rustic resort is a good choice for families and nature-lovers. Spacious, airy cabins have ceiling fans or air-conditioning. There's a saltwater pool, tidal pools to explore, and grassy areas to play in.

La Paloma Lodge

Drake Bay; tel: 2293-7502; www. lapalomalodge.com; $$$$ (all-inclusive)

On a breezy ocean bluff, this romantic lodge is set in a lush, bird-filled tropical garden. Spacious air-conditioned cabins have sea and jungle views. Excellent meals are at convivial communal tables and afternoon tea is served with home-baked treats. Tours include snorkeling, diving, and whale- and dolphin-watching. The coastal path starts at the lodge entrance.

Osa Peninsula

Puerto Jiménez
Bosque del Río Tigre

Dos Brazos del Tigre, 12km (7.5 miles) west of Puerto Jiménez; tel: 8705-3729 (text message); www.bosquedelriotigre.com; $$$ (all-inclusive)

This rustic, riverside eco-lodge is bird-watcher heaven, set in a private preserve. Four open-air rooms with comfortable mosquito-netted beds share bathrooms and garden hot-water showers. A separate cabin in the woods has private bath and shower. Rates include three gourmet meals and tours with the best birding guide on the peninsula.

Cabinas Jiménez

Waterfront, Puerto Jiménez; tel: 2735-5090; www.cabinasjimenez.com; $

The coolest rooms in town have air-conditioning, fridges, coffeemakers, and a gulf view. There's guarded parking, a small plunge pool, and a family-size casita. No meals, but restaurants are a short walk away. The friendly American owner runs boat cruises and fishing trips.

Iguana Lodge

Playa Platanares, 4km (2.5 miles) south of Puerto Jiménez; tel: 2206-5859; http://iguanalodge.com; $$$ (all-inclusive)

Elegant suites in beachfront, two-story cabins set in a lush garden. Candlelit dining brings guests together for international buffets. Lap pool, and the Golfo Dulce waves are gentle enough for swimming. Practice yoga here or on the beach and relax at the spa.

Matapalo
Bosque del Cabo

22km (14 miles) south of Puerto Jiménez; tel: 8389-2846; www.bosquedelcabo.com; $$$$ (all-inclusive)

Birdwatching, Finca Exotica eco-lodge

Romantic bungalows have garden showers and ocean or garden views set in hundreds of hectares of primary forest. Four villas come fully equipped for families. There are two pools, plus yoga sessions, and a spa. Excellent naturalist guides lead bird-watching and wildlife tours.

El Remanso

Matapalo, 22km (14 miles) south of Puerto Jiménez; tel: 2735-5569; www.elremanso. com; $$$$ (all-inclusive)

Sophisticated and serene, this eco-lodge is in primary forest, with a small pool and nature trail down to a beach with tidal pools. Lofty bungalows have modern furnishings. There's a romantic terrace restaurant shaded by palm trees. A popular tour involves rappelling down waterfalls.

Lapa Ríos

20km (12 miles) south of Puerto Jiménez; tel: 2735 -5130; www.laparios.com; $$$$ (all-inclusive)

Each thatch-roofed bungalow at this eco-lodge has a private garden and outdoor shower where toucans and monkeys visit. Resident naturalist guides lead tours through the rain forest. An infinity pool overlooks the forest with Golfo Dulce views. Superb meals, tours, and transportation to the lodge are included.

Carate
Finca Exotica

Carate, across from landing strip; tel: 4070-0054; www.fincaexotica.com; $$ (all-inclusive)

Indonesian-style cabins and safari tents offer an alternative, low-key style of natural luxury in a tropical garden that also supplies organic produce to the rancho restaurant. The focus here is on simplicity and sustainability, with collective, healthy meals, and yoga. Minimum stay three nights.

Luna Lodge

2km (1 mile) from Carate along river bed and up steep hill; tel: 4070-0010; http://lunalodge.com; $$$$ (all-inclusive)

Round cabins have panoramic views at this mountaintop eco-lodge and yoga retreat, with a spa and tree-shaded pool. Buffet dinners in the rancho restaurant feature local fish plus vegetarian options. The forest has a steep trail to a waterfall. A 4X4 vehicle is essential.

Golfo Dulce
Playa Cativo Lodge

Golfo Dulce, by boat from Puerto Jiménez or Golfito; playacativo.com; $$$$ (all-inclusive)

This eco-lodge fuses high design, deluxe comforts, and fine cuisine to create the ideal romantic lodge. The three-story lodge has five spacious, sophisticated suites with panoramic views and stunning bathrooms. A secluded screened-in cottage for two sits closer to the shore. Palm-fringed beach, freshwater pool, and forest trails.

Playa Nicuesa Rainforest Lodge

Across Golfo Dulce, by boat from Puerto Jiménez; tel: 2258-8250; www.nicuesalodge.com; $$$$ (all-inclusive)

Hacienda Alta Gracia   *Casa Botania*

This eco-lodge with its own beach and forest has adventures on land along forest trails, and on sea, in kayaks, sailboats, and fishing boats. Relax with yoga on the beach or a massage. Excellent meals. Beautifully crafted wood bungalows are scattered around the lush garden.

Road to Chirripó
El Pelicano Mountain Hotel
San Gerardo de Rivas; tel: 2742-5050; www.hotelpelicano.net; $

Simple rooms with private bath come with a ride to the Chirripó trailhead for hikers. Guests who want to bird-watch or relax and enjoy the mountain views can opt for private cabins around a swimming pool. The folk-art museum here is unique.

Río Chirripó Retreat
San Gerardo de Rivas; tel: 2742-5109; riochirripo.com; $$

Paths through a spectacular tropical garden lead to the river spilling over rocks. Rooms in a two-story building are comfortable, with balconies overlooking the river; suites and a river cabin for two are more private. Yoga is the main event here, every morning at 8am ($15). Breakfast and dinner are in the temple-like main building.

Talari Lodge
Route 242, 5km (3 miles) east of Inter-American Highway; tel: 2771-0341; www.talari.co.cr; $

Birds abound along forest and river trails at this nature lodge with modest but comfortable cabins. There's a swimming pool and covered tennis courts. Meals are light and healthy, served in a pleasant, open-air restaurant with bird-feeders providing entertainment.

San Isidro de El General
Hacienda Alta Gracia
Santa Teresa de Cajón, 20km (12.5 miles) south of San Isidro de El General; tel: 2105-3000; www.aubergeresorts.com; $$$$

This glamorous hilltop resort has ultra-luxurious suites and *casitas*, beautifully landscaped grounds, a stable with horses to ride, a pool with a view, and a spa. Chefs prepare haute cuisine in an open kitchen. Guests can fly by private plane to the hotel's landing strip.

San Vito
Casa Botania
5km (3 miles) south of San Vito; tel: 2773-4217; www.casabotania.com; $

Rooms with a view at this charming B&B come with bountiful breakfasts. Suites with artisan wood furnishings have balconies. The co-owner is a naturalist guide and his Belgian wife is the genius behind elegant fish and vegetarian dinners.

Cascata del Bosco
Across from Wilson Botanical Gardens, San Vito; tel: 2773-3208; www.cascatadelbosco.com; $

So close to the botanical garden, this property attracts birds and birders. Unique round cottages with balconies are equipped with coffeemakers and fridges.

A cosy corner at Villa Blanca Cloud Forest Hotel

Hearty Tico and American-style breakfasts. The bar is popular with expats.

San Ramón
Villa Blanca Cloud Forest Hotel
20km (12 miles) north of San Ramón; tel: 2461-0300; www.villablanca-costarica.com; $$$$

High in the clouds, this upscale hotel has whitewashed *casitas* modeled on traditional country houses, with romantic fireplaces and bathtubs for two. There's a movie theatre and even a wedding chapel. Naturalist guides lead tours through the cloud forest.

Arenal

Arenal Kioro Suites & Spa
10km (6 miles) east of La Fortuna; tel: 2479-1700; www.hotelarenalkioro.com; $$$$

This modern, luxury hotel has a string of 53 spacious suites with volcano views. Each has two balconies, Jacuzzi, widescreen TV, and air conditioning. There's a private hot spring, a swimming pool, and two restaurants and bars.

Arenal Observatory Lodge
8km (5 miles) south, off Route 142, on dirt road to El Castillo; tel: 2479-1070; www.arenalobservatorylodge.com; $$

This hotel is as close as you can get to the volcano. Resident guides lead daily tours through the immaculate gardens and forest trails, full of birds. Rooms are comfortable and staffers are helpful. Buffet breakfast on the terrace with views of the volcano and Lake Arenal.

Arenal Volcano Lake Lodge
Beside church in La Unión, 10km (6 miles) east of Nuevo Arenal; tel: 2692-8100; www.arenalvolcanolakehotel.com; $

This motel-style lodge overlooking the lake is a bargain. Rooms for two have king-size beds and family rooms have a bunk and two single beds. The amiable host speaks English and arranges tours. Breakfast comes with a lake view.

Cabinas Los Guayabos
9km (5.5 miles) east of La Fortuna; tel: 2479-1444; www.cabinaslosguayabos.com; $

With the same volcano views as Kioro, the bargain rooms here are in pretty, duplex terracotta cottages with garden terraces facing the volcano. No. 6 is a little more private. No meals or credit cards.

Tabacón Grand Spa Thermal Resort
13km (8 miles) west of La Fortuna; tel: 2479-2000; www.tabacon.com; $$$$

This large luxury hotel (over 100 rooms and suites) gives guests special access, early morning and late afternoon, to the thermal springs running through the resort's landscaped gardens. There's also a spa and romantic restaurant. Minimum stay two nights.

Villa Decary
2km (1 mile) east of Nuevo Arenal; tel: 2694-4330; www.villadecary.com; $$

On a hilltop overlooking Lake Arenal, this B&B is famous for its lavish breakfasts and friendly American hosts. Each

Arenal Observatory Lodge – it doesn't get closer than this

comfortably furnished bungalow has picture windows and a terrace with a lake view. Bird-watch from your terrace or hike the property's forest trails. There's also a hilltop yoga studio.

Monteverde

Arco-Iris Eco-Lodge

Downtown Santa Elena; tel: 2645-5067; www.arcoirislodge.com; $$

This in-town eco-lodge still maintains a country feeling, surrounded by 1.6 hectares (4 acres) of forest with excellent birding trails. Wooden cabins range from small ones with bunk beds to two-story superiors with queen beds. Breakfast not included, but it's a short walk to cafés.

Hotel Belmar

4km (2.5 miles) north of Monteverde Reserve; tel: 2645-5201; www.hotelbelmar. net; $$$

Atop a steep hill, this 22-room, chalet-style hotel is pure elegance. Rooms gleam with polished wood and balconies have views to the Gulf of Nicoya (there are no TVs in rooms). The upscale restaurant uses organic produce from the hotel's own farm, and the terrace bar is popular at sunset. Yoga classes are gratis. Breakfast not included.

Los Pinos

200 meters/yds east of Cerro Plano School; tel: 2645-5252; www.lospinos.net; $$

This hillside private preserve with 16 cabins tucked into forest and gardens has hiking trails, abundant wildlife, and

a hydroponic garden where you can purchase vegetables and herbs. Cabins range from a cozy wood cottage for two, to three-bedroom, three-bathroom family houses with kitchens.

Nosara

Boutique Hotel Lagarta Lodge

North end of Nosara; tel: 2682-0035; www.lagartalodge.com; $$$

This hilltop lodge with an eagle's-eye view of the ocean sits atop a private mangrove preserve. Spacious new suites have air-conditioning, picture windows, and terraces. Bird-watching is the main event, along with cooling off in two swimming pools. There's a romantic terrace for cocktails and spectacular sunsets.

Casa Romantica Hotel

Left down road at Giardino Tropicale, to Playa Guiones; tel: 2682-0272; www.casa-romantica.net; $$

This aptly named small hotel in the Spanish-colonial-style is just steps from the beach, along a shaded path. A large swimming pool sits in a lovely garden. The alfresco restaurant serves European cuisine with tropical touches. Rooms are spacious and some have air-conditioning.

Harmony Hotel

Road to Playa Guiones; tel: 2682-4114; www.harmonynosara.com; $$$$

The area's most sustainable and luxurious hotel has a native-plant garden, organic cuisine, yoga classes, and a

new-age spa. Guests enjoy a lovely pool and access via a shaded path directly to the beach. Rooms facing the pool aren't large but they are elegant, with private gardens. Larger suites and bungalows are closest to the beach.

Playa Sámara
Hotel Belvedere

One block east of Main Street on road to Playa Carrillo; tel: 2656-0213; www.belvederesamara.net; $

A great option for longer stays, this hilltop hotel has coffeemakers, air-conditioning, fridges in sparse but immaculate rooms and suites, some with terrace views. It's a 10-minute walk down to the beach, but with two pools and a large garden, you may not leave. There's a separate honeymoon cottage in the back garden. Breakfast not included.

Hotel Giada

Playa Sámara main road; tel: 2636-0132; www.hotelgiada.net; $

The pick of Sámara's boutique hotels, this Italian-owned, affordable hotel a block from the beach has balconies festooned with fuschia bougainvillea, overlooking two small pools. The casually chic rooms have bamboo furniture and colorful Guatemalan textiles. The restaurant serves excellent pizza and tiramisú.

Villas Playa Sámara

Off main road to Carrillo, 2km (1.2 mile) south of Sámara; tel: 2656-1111; https://villasplayasamara.com; $$$

For a beach vacation, you can't beat these equipped one- and two-bedroom villas steps from the superb beach. Less expensive rooms are farther from the beach, near the huge swimming pool, restaurant, and spa. Sámara and its restaurants are a 15-minute, scenic walk along the beach.

Punta Islita
Hotel Punta Islita

Punta Islita, 16km (11 miles) east of Playa Carrillo; tel: 2656-2020; www.hotelpuntaislita.com; $$$$

These secluded, hilltop luxury suites and villas have sweeping Pacific views from its upscale restaurant, fronted by an infinity pool, plus a beach club and large pool down by the rocky shore. The spa is luxurious and service is impeccable.

Caribbean Coast

Cahuita
Atlántida Lodge

North of soccer field, on beach road, Cahuita; tel: 2755-0115; www.atlantidalodgecahuita.com; $

Giant sculptures of toucans and frogs signal the entrance to this lodge with 32 modest rooms in duplex cabins and two suites, close to the beach. Dense jungle makes the rooms, without air-conditioning, rather dark and warm. Large swimming pool and lively bar/restaurant.

El Encanto Hotel & Spa

Playa Negra road, 200 meters/yds west of Cahuita Main Street; tel: 2755-0113;

www.elencantocahuita.com; $$
Luxurious rooms, suites, and bungalows are enclosed in a Zen garden across the road from the black-sand beach. Breakfasts are served on elegant white china. There's a pool and a discreet Jacuzzi and massage area.

Magellan Boutique Hotel
Playa Viquez, 2km (1.2 miles) north of Cahuita; tel: 2755-0035; www.magellanboutiquehotel.com; $$
This upscale B&B has six freshly decorated rooms with king-size beds, air-conditioning, tiled bathrooms, and small fridges. A yoga studio adds even more serenity to the palm-shaded garden. Breakfasts offer four choices.

Puerto Viejo
Cariblue Beach & Jungle Resort
Playa Cocles, 2km (1.2 mile) south of Puerto Viejo; tel: 2750-0035; www.cariblue.com; $$
This Italian-chic couples resort has 23 air-conditioned, thatch-roofed bungalows, and 12 rooms and 8 suites all with terraces in a lush garden, a minute's walk to the beach. There's a pool and a hot tub. Lavish breakfast buffet; Italian menu the rest of the day.

Casa Verde Lodge
200 meters/yds east of bus stop; tel: 2750-0015; www.casaverdelodge.com; $
Fresh, bright rooms at this in-town lodge on a quiet side street have polished wood floors, ceiling fans or air-conditioning, and balconies with hammocks overlooking a mature garden with a pool and tiny frogs. Breakfast not included.

Escape Caribeño
On the beach, opposite the Salsa Brava surf break; tel: 2750-0103; www.escapecaribeno.com; $ (taxes not included)
These 14 wood bungalows are comfortable, air-conditioned, and affordable. Tiled bathrooms and polished wood interiors are immaculate. Paths lead through the garden to the beach with tidal pools. Breakfast is extra but it's a short walk to town and its cafés.

Physis B&B
Off main road, Playa Cocles; tel: 2750-0491; http://physiscaribbean.net; $$
Three fresh and pretty rooms with immaculate en-suite bathrooms and one very private honeymoon cottage are enclosed in an enchanting garden oasis. There's air-conditioning, Wi-Fi, and cable TV. The bountiful breakfast features every imaginable tropical fruit and hot dishes prepared to order by an amiable host.

Manzanillo
Almonds & Corals
Near end of paved road to Manzanillo; tel: 2759-9056; www.almondsandcorals.com; $$
Rough it in style, perched in a spacious, comfortable tent in the treetops, with a canopy bed, en-suite bathroom, and a wake-up call from howler monkeys. A wooden walkway leads to a totally private beach, with roofed-over hammocks lined up on the sand.

RESTAURANTS

Eating out in Costa Rica can entail a bewildering range of experiences. One day, you may find yourself in a tree house eating fried whole trout you just caught yourself, and the next night you could be dining in a chic temple of gastronomy, sampling complicated fusion cuisine.

While San José and its suburbs are home to most of the high-end restaurants and outposts of international chains, there are also pockets of gastronomy in the hinterlands, notably Monteverde and Arenal in the Northwest; Dominical, Uvita, and Ojochal in the South Pacific; and the Caribbean coast.

Prices

Prices run the gamut from $5 for a filling lunch in a simple soda (family-run café) to $100 in a stylish San José or resort-hotel restaurant.

Officially, menus should include final prices, including the government-dictated 13 percent tax plus 10 percent service charge. But many high-end restaurants do not include those taxes in their menu price, so look out for the small print at the bottom of the menu.

Be aware of the true pricing when comparing menus before you choose a restaurant. An extra 23 percent can add a considerable amount to the cost of your meal. Some menus in high-tourist areas may also be denominated in US dollars, adding another level of confusion in comparing prices.

Tipping and service

By law, servers are supposed to receive the 10 percent service tax, so there is no expectation of a tip. But if a server has been extra helpful or friendly, do leave a small cash tip that you know will go directly to them.

In most restaurants, no one will hurry you out by presenting the bill. You are expected to ask for the bill when you are ready to leave.

With those caveats in mind, enjoy your meal, or as Costa Ricans say: "Buen provecho!"

A glass of expensive, imported wine with dinner is not common. Local beer and fruit drinks are the beverages of choice. These prices reflect the cost of a main dish with a local beverage.
$ = Under $10
$$ = $10–$15
$$$ = $15–$20
$$$$ = Over $20

San José

Grano de Oro

Calle 30, Avenida 2-4; tel: 2255-3322; www.hotelgranodeoro.com; daily 7am–10pm; $$$$
The reigning queen of San José dining combines sumptuous high-Victorian

Delicate flavors

decor with haute Costa Rican and international cuisine. The kitchen is famous for velvety pejibaye soup and decadent desserts. Courtyard tables around a fountain are perfect for lunch, afternoon tea, or a romantic dinner. Service is polished and friendly.

Kalú

Calle 31, corner of Avenida 5, Barrio Escalante; tel: 2253-8426; www.kalu.co.cr; Tue–Sat noon–10pm, no dinner Sun; $$
The hippest restaurant in town is perfect for a lavish brunch, light lunch, or romantic dinner. The contemporary menu melds Tico, Italian, Thai, and American flavors. Sampler dinner menus, designed for couples, pair three mains with three different wines. The chef is a master *pâtissier*, so don't skip dessert.

Lubnan

Paseo Colón, between calles 22 and 24; tel: 2257-6071; Tue–Sat 11am–3pm and 6–midnight, Sun 11am–5pm (no dinner); $$
Come hungry and willing to share huge platters of excellent Mid-eastern mezze. Vegetarians will appreciate the hummus and grain choices. The tapestry-hung bar is popular, especially during Thursday-night's belly-dancing show.

Park Café

100 meters/yds north of Rosti Pollo, Sabana Norte; tel: 2290-6324; www.parkcafecostarica.blogspot.com; Tue–Sat noon–2.30pm, Wed–Fri 7–9pm; closed Sep–Oct; $$$

Innovative, exotic dishes served in tapas-sized portions continually delight and are changed frequently by the Michelin-starred British chef. Tables are on a covered terrace filled with Balinese antiques, or, in good weather, in the romantic garden. No children, in deference to the antiques.

Whapin'

200 meters/yds east of El Farolito (lighthouse), barrio Escalante; tel: 2283-1480; 11.30am–2.30pm and 6–10pm; $$
In case you skip the Caribbean coast, here's your chance to sample authentic Afro-Caribbean red beans and coconut rice served in a funky, island-style restaurant with a bar that opens onto the sidewalk. Try the fried breadfruit when it's in season and enjoy the reggae soundtrack. (Whapin' is short for 'What's Happening?')

Escazú

Chez Christophe

Across from Centro Comercial Paco; tel: 2228-2512; Tue–Sun 7am–7pm; $
If you're craving a buttery croissant instead of tortillas, the best French bakery in the Central Valley also serves light lunches and early suppers, featuring creative salads, omelettes, and smoked-salmon baguette sandwiches. The pains au chocolat will transport you to France.

Di Bartolo Ristorante e Enoteca

850 meters/yds north of Centro Comercial Paco, Guachipélin Road; tel: 2288-6787;

Tue–Sat 10am–11pm, Sun noon–6pm; $$$$

From carpaccio to caprese salad to shared calamari starters, this elegant, Tuscan-inspired restaurant is authentically Italian. You can splurge on superb veal Marsala or stay within a modest budget and share a starter and an excellent pizza, with a glass of Italian wine from the vast wine cellar. Save room for the ricotta tart with fresh strawberries or the chocolate cake with a creamy Nutella center.

Santa Ana

Bacchus

300 meters/yds north of Montes gas station; tel: 2282-5441; Tue–Sat noon–3pm and 6–10pm; $$$

Excellent Mediterranean fare is served in a chic, restored historical house decorated with modern art and on an adjoining garden patio. Along with refined French and Italian fare, there's affordable pizza and an extensive wine list.

La Luz Restaurant & Bar

Hotel Alta Las Palomas, east side of Santa Ana; tel: 2282-4160; www.thealtahotel.com; daily 6.30am–10pm; $$$$

For a very special occasion splurge at this chic, glass-fronted restaurant with a view, serving an innovative fusion of organic, exotic, and tropical cuisine. Start with a cream of ayote (pumpkin) soup with lemongrass and ginger, or sautéed shrimp with mango and spices. Reservations advised.

Heredia

Casa Antigua Café & Restaurant

San Josécito; 1km (0.6 mile) east of San Isidro de Heredia; Sat–Sun 8am–8pm; $

There aren't many vestiges of Victorian times left in Costa Rica, but Casa Antigua Café & Restaurante in San Josécito occupies a carefully restored hacienda, formerly the center of a large coffee plantation. It's worth visiting for its exuberant, faux-painted, spindled-wood decor. Stop in for coffee and cake, a cool cerveza, or a light lunch.

Dominical

Café Mono Congo

Pueblo del Río, Main Street; tel: 8485-5523; daily 6.30am–9pm; $

Creative vegetarian and gluten-free dishes at this hip riverside café are delicious enough that you can forget about what's missing. Espresso and cappuccino are full strength and the Chocolate Papaya Pie is addictive. Herbal teas, kombucha, and organic juices have no caffeine and craft beer is on tap.

Phat Noodle

Main Street, across from Pueblo del Río; tel: 2787-0017; Mon 5–9pm, Tue–Sun 11am–9pm; $$

Prepare your taste buds for spicy Pad Thai and savory Indonesian satays and curries at this covered, outdoor restaurant with a youthful vibe. Service is at polished-wood tables and the kitchen is in a converted truck. Daily lunch specials include a noodle dish and fruit

Veggie-heaven Café Mono Congo

smoothie for less than $10. The signature cocktail is a jalapeño-spiced pineapple margarita. Craft beers are on tap.

Por Qué No?

Seafront; tel: 2787-0340; www.costaparaiso.com; Tue–Sun 7am–9pm; $$$

For romance, you can't beat this pricey but scenic oceanfront restaurant. Start with cocktails on the sunset deck perched on the rocky shoreline, then move to the upper terrace to dine on red snapper in an almond crust, fish tacos with mango sauce, or a wood-fired pizza. You can also catch early-morning sun here for breakfast.

Tortilla Flats

Dominical Beach; tel: 2787-0033; daily 8am–10pm; $$

California-style baguette sandwiches, Mexican fare, and fresh fish specials on the menu, surf videos playing on big screens, and margaritas and flavored daiquiris shaken up at the bar all contribute to the happy beach-bar vibe here. And it all comes with a great view of buff surfers and sunbathers strolling past.

Uvita

Sabor Español

Bahía Ballena road, south of Uvita, follow signs along dirt road; tel: 8768-9160; Tue–Sun 6–9.30pm, closed Sep 15–Dec 15; $$

It's worth the drive on a bumpy dirt road to this intimate, rancho restaurant for the authentic Catalan cuisine,

including paella, spicy gazpacho, whisky-flambéed shrimp, or chicken in a mango rum sauce. Sangria comes by the pitcher. Reservations are a must since there are only six or so tables. No credit cards.

Villa Leonor

Between Km 170 and 171 on Costanera, Bahía Ballena; tel: 2786-5380; Mon, Wed–Sat 11am–8pm, Sun 11am–6pm; $$

Chicken and fish fajitas are favorites at this lively rancho restaurant, just steps from the beach. Kids can jump in the swimming pool while adults enjoy tropical cocktails at the swim-up bar. On weekends, there's a popular BBQ brunch, and garlic-buttery lobsters can be ordered ahead. No credit cards.

Ojochal

The Bamboo Room

Alma de Ojochal Hotel, left turn 400 meters/yds south of Ojochal, off Costanera; tel: 2786-5295; Mon–Sat noon–10pm; $$

Breezy, with ocean and jungle views, this open-air restaurant serves a signature, big-enough-to-share, exotic BamBOOM salad with panko-crusted shrimp, and divine beer-battered fish and crisp chips. Ice creams are homemade, flavoured with coconuts, dates, and rum. The restaurant rocks, literally, with nightly live music (see page 125).

Exotica Restaurant

Main road in Ojochal, 300 meters/yds past the yellow bridge; tel: 2786-5050; Mon–Sat

5–10pm by reservation only; $$$
This romantic, patio restaurant under a thatch roof is acclaimed for its menu of classic French cuisine with tropical accents. Start with a Spicy Vietnamese chicken soup or Tahitian fish carpaccio with bananas. Change continents with duck breast *à l'orange*. Presentation is exquisite and desserts include flourless chocolate cake, dark and peppery; or tangy passion-fruit ice cream with mora (blackberry) coulis.

La Fortuna
Don Rufino
On Route 142, two blocks east of the church in La Fortuna; tel: 2479-9997; daily 11am–11pm; $$$
Carnivore heaven, this upscale, macho steakhouse charbroils beef, pork ribs, and even lamb sirloin to perfection. Interesting sides are delicious (and suitable for vegetarians), including butternut squash purée, wilted spinach, and purple corn polenta. Jumbo shrimps and fish also hit the coals. The bar is open to the street and is popular with local expats.

Nuevo Arenal
Gingerbread Fine Dining
1.5km (2 miles) east of Nuevo Arenal; tel: 2694-0039; www.gingerbreadarenal.com; Tue–Sat 5–9pm; $$$$
Reserve ahead for dinner at this exciting, if eccentric, restaurant. The larger-than-life Israeli chef changes the menu daily depending on what's fresh, but you can usually count on gargantuan portions of exquisitely prepared pork, ribs, filet mignon, shrimp, and fish, paired with wines from an extensive cellar. Macadamia cheesecake is a dessert hit. Prices are high, but mains are big enough to share. No credit cards.

Monteverde
Restaurante Arrecifes
Cerro Plano, 50 meters/yds north of the school; tel: 2645-7158; daily 11am–10pm; $$
Formerly known as El Márquez in Santa Elena, this new incarnation in Cerro Plano is just as popular but much more spacious. It's not fancy but the same family cooks and serves the same excellent fish and seafood at reasonable prices. The ceviche is fresh and tangy, the seafood pasta more generous than most appetites can handle, and the *corvina* (sea bass) in a tropical fruit sauce is heavenly.

Sofía
On road to Butterfly Garden, Cerro Plano; tel: 2645-7017; daily 11.30am–9.30pm; $$$
Innovative "new Latin" fare is served in three small dining rooms at this stylish, upscale restaurant. Chicken with a guava reduction, the crusted corvina (sea bass), and curried mango-chutney shrimp top the menu favorites. For dessert there is a meltingly delicious chocolate chimichanga (fried pastry roll), served with choco-

Stashu's Con Fusion

late ice cream that keeps customers coming back for more.

Puerto Jiménez

Corcovado Marisquería, Restaurante y Bar

On the waterfront, across from dock; tel: 2735-5659; daily 7am–11pm; $

The main draws at this very casual, alfresco spot are the Golfo views and breezes, plus a huge selection of seafood appetizers at very affordable prices, served at picnic tables shaded by palm trees. The extensive menu includes ceviche, a generous arroz con camarones (fried rice with shrimp) and even grilled lobsters (when available) and non-fishy grilled sirloin steak.

Puerto Viejo de Talamanca

Amimodo

South Main Street, Puerto Viejo; tel: 2750-0257; daily noon–10pm; $$

Dine on classic Northern Italian cuisine with a tropical accent at candle-lit tables set out on the sand, or on the verandah of the gingerbread-trimmed house. Homemade lobster ravioli is a standout. Or try the exotic ravioli version stuffed with shrimp, pineapple, coconut, ginger, and curry.

Chile Rojo

South Main Street, across from market stands; tel: 2750-0421; Mon, Thu–Sun 11.30am–11pm, Wed 11.30am–10pm; $$

Exotic flavors include spicy Thai, Middle Eastern, and East Indian at this vegetarian and vegan-friendly restaurant. Thai-spiced grilled tuna is a favorite. An all-you-can-eat sushi buffet brings in a crowd on Monday nights, along with two-for-one drink specials.

Stashus con Fusion

South Main Street; tel: 2750-0530; Thu–Tue 5–10pm; $$

Exotic fusion is all the rage at this energetically organic, dinner-only establishment. First you choose from chicken, marlin, tuna, shrimp, or vegetables and then select a topping sauce from an international roster of Thai, Indonesian, Mexican, Jamaican, or Malaysian. On Sunday nights there's sometimes live music into the night.

Playa Cocles

La Pecora Nera

Across from Panadería Frances, Playa Cocles; tel: 2750-0490; Tue–Sun 5–10pm; $$$$

The best Italian restaurant in the country is this elegant, thatched-roof rancho lit with fairy lights and backed by a soft jazz soundtrack. Step into the wine cave to taste and choose your wine. On the changing menu a creamy red-snapper soup with shrimp ravioli, carpaccio of tuna, and chicken stuffed with prosciutto regularly feature. Mains arrive with five small plates of sides and a basket of three just-baked breads. Finish with classic tiramisú or chocolatey profiteroles. Service is as polished as the cuisine.

Jazz Café performance

NIGHTLIFE

San José has a smattering of live-performance venues. But most entertainment in tourist areas is in sports bars with DJs and recorded rock, salsa, and merengue music, along with karaoke.

Some downtown bars are dingy dens for drugs and prostitution, which is legal in Costa Rica. If the place looks seedy, it probably is. El Pueblo, a complex of bars and restaurants on the east side of town, is fine during the day but its narrow, winding alleyways can be dangerous at night.

Also, best to order only bottled drinks at bars and watch them being opened.

San José

Ram Luna

14.5km (9 miles) south of San José; 5km (3 miles) from Aserri on the road to Tarbaca; tel: 2230-3022; www.restauranteramluna.com
This lively restaurant puts on a memorable dinner show of mariachis, acoustic guitar music, and folk dancing, Wednesday and Thursday. Transportation can be arranged. Reserve ahead.

Castro's Bar & Disco

200 meters/yds west of Cuerpo de Bomberos, Barrio Mexico; tel: 2256-8789; www.castrosbar.wixsite.com/castros
If you want to dance to Latin rhythms or just watch the locals dance up a storm, head to this large club. It opens at 6pm and often goes till 4am. Take a taxi since it's not easy to find your way there.

El Observatorio

Across from Cine Magaly in Barrio California; tel: 2223-0725; https://elobservatorio.tv
This hip club often has live music, karaoke, and stand-up comedy.

Jazz Café

Avenida Centrale next to Banco Popular in San Pedro; tel: 2253-8933; www.jazzcafecostarica.com
The focus at this intimate jazz club is on live jazz, Monday through Saturday nights. But you can also catch live performances ranging from rock to R&B to funk.

La Avispa

Calle 1, Avenida 8; tel: 2223-5343; www.laavispa.com
This popular LGBTQ venue is open Thursday to Sunday nights, with dance floors, karaoke, and pool tables.

Escazú

8ova (Octavo Rooftop)

Top floor of the Sheraton Hotel; tel: 4055-0505
You'll find a mix of glitz, cocktails, live music on weekends, and a night-owl's view of city lights from this high perch.

Henry's Beach Café

200 meters/yds north of Centro Comercial Paco; tel: 2289-6250; www.henrysbeachcafe.com
This open-air restaurant bar usually has music and a convivial crowd.

A lot of dancing happens at Coco's Bar

Jazz Café's Escazú branch

Off the main highway, in front of CIMA Hospital; tel: 2288-4740
Check the weekly live music schedule at www.jazzcafecostarica.com.

Arenal

La Fortuna
Lava Lounge Bar & Grill

West of the church in downtown La Fortuna; tel: 2479-7365; www.lavaloungecostarica.com
This club advertises itself as the 'hot spot' under the Arenal volcano, with live music Wednesday and Saturday nights.

South Pacific

Dominical
Fuego Brew Co

Off Main Street, south of Catholic Church; tel: 8992-9559; www.fuegobrew.com
There's live music almost every night at this hip, lively open-air restaurant/ lounge bar/brewery.

Roca Verde

1km (0.6 mile) south of Dominical, off the Costanera Highway; tel: 2787-0036; www.rocaverde.net
Every Friday night, bluesy rock band Ben' Jammin and the Howlers, led by virtuoso jazz fiddler Nancy Buchan, rock the joint.

Ojochal
The Bamboo Room

Alma Hotel, Ojochal; tel: 2786-5295; www.almacr.com
There's live music nightly, Monday to Saturday, aimed at a mature crowd and fans of classic rock, acoustic guitar, and folk-rock.

Caribbean

Cahuita
Coco's Bar

Main Street; tel: 2755-0437
Just follow the reggae and Latin beats emanating from this bar on weekends and look for dancers in the street.

The Reggae Bar

50 meters/yds north of the soccer field; tel: 2755-0209
This casual, slightly raucous bar delivers the signature sound of the Caribbean. Call ahead to check what's on.

Puerto de Viejo
Hot Rocks

80 meters/yds west of ATEC; no phone
This breezy bar close to the beach has live music, karaoke, and open-mike.

Mango Sunset

20 meters/yds south of main Puerto Viejo bus stop; tel: 8691-0756
Beach bar with music 6pm–midnight.

Manzanillo
Maxi's

On the beach; tel: 2759-9073
Reggae and Latin beats blare out from this popular restaurant's downstairs bar.

A–Z

A

Addresses

Streets have numbers but buildings do not, so 'addresses' often rely on relationships to recognizable landmarks: for example 200 meters/yds west of Hotel Don Carlos (100 meters/yds denotes one city block).

In San José and other towns, there's a four-part grid system, with a central *avenida* (Av.) running east and west; and a central Calle (Ca.) running north and south. *Avenidas* have odd numbers north of central avenue, even numbers south. For *calles*, even numbers are to the west of *Calle Centrale*; odd numbers to the east.

Narrowing down a location is expressed by relationships, as in Calle Central, Avenida 2–4. The first part is the street or avenue on which the building is located; the second part indicates the streets or avenues the building is between. An 'address' may also include a *barrio* (neighborhood) name, to help you zero in on the correct area.

Age restrictions

You must be 18 to drink or drive in Costa Rica. To rent a car, you must be over 21. A recent law raised the age of sexual consent from 16 to 18, and the marriageable age to 18.

B

Budgeting

Many visitors find Costa Rica more expensive than they expected. Away from the cities and resort areas, you can still find bargains, especially in family-run, local restaurants and lodges.

Eating: A bottle of domestic beer, or a *caña* (draft) in a local bar or café costs $2. Watch for two-for-one specials at happy hour. Micro-brewed, craft beers will cost more, around $6. A glass of house wine, usually Chilean and Argentinian, costs $5 to $6. European wines in higher-end restaurants will set you back $8 and more.

A hearty lunchtime *casado* in a budget *soda* costs between $5 and $7. Count on spending $10 to $12 dollars for a main course in a seaside café. In resort hotels and upscale international restaurants, prices are steeper, $15 to $20 for a main dish, up to $30 for steak or seafood.

Lodging: A basic cabin for two, with *agua corriente* (ambient-temperature water) private bath, can cost as little as $30. But a more comfortable cabin, with hot-water shower, will run $50 to $75, depending on location and time of year. Boutique and deluxe resort hotels can range from $150 to $700.

Getting around: A taxi from the airport to downtown San José costs between $25 and $35. City bus fares are usually

Fun on the beach

less than $1 per ride, but there are no transfers. Long-distance buses are the biggest bargain; you can travel from San José, for example, all the way to Puerto Jiménez in the southern Osa Peninsula for less than $15.

C

Children

Costa Ricans adore children and they're welcome almost everywhere. Most all-inclusive hotels offer kids' clubs and activity programs, as well as babysitting. However, children under 12 are often not welcome in hotels geared to romantic getaways or serene yoga retreats.

Babes in arms are fairly easy to travel with, although parents may have difficulty sterilizing bottles and finding baby supplies in remote communities. Most city streets and country areas are not stroller-friendly.

Clothing

Pack as lightly as possible and plan to dress in layers, with a sweater or light jacket for cool evenings, especially at higher altitudes. Nothing beats light cotton for comfort and coolness in the tropics. Avoid denim jeans – they will be hot and uncomfortable and, once wet, they will never dry.

It rains a lot in the tropics, so bring closed, waterproof hiking shoes and many pairs of socks. Sandals, even the hiking types, are not advised for forest trails.

The sun in strong: bring a wide-brimmed sun hat that covers neck and ears. Shorts are worn everywhere, even in the city, but on forest trails, you are better off wearing loose, long pants that can be tucked into your socks, to avoid biting insects and stinging thorns, and long-sleeved, loose shirts.

Crime and safety

Opportunistic theft is a problem. Pickpocketing and backpack grabbing are, for the most part, non-violent, snatch-and-run crimes, but there are some instances of theft at knifepoint and very occasionally at gunpoint.

You don't have to be paranoid but you do have to be vigilant. Avoid deserted streets at night and isolated areas.

The best way to reduce losses is to leave non-essential valuables, especially jewelry, back home. When you're out, carry only the cash you need and one credit card. Leave the rest, along with your passport, locked in your room safety box or the hotel office.

The most common thefts occur on what appear to be deserted beaches. Always leave someone attending towels, backpacks, and camping gear. Don't take anything of value to the beach, especially wallets or passports.

Report thefts immediately to the Judicial Investigative Police (OIJ, pronounced oh-ee-ho-ta) if your passport is stolen or you need a police report for insurance.

Colorful scarves and dresses for sale at a market

Customs regulations

You can bring personal effects into the country, plus 500g (18oz) of tobacco, 2kg (4lbs) of candy and 5liters (170 fl. oz) of liquor (if you're over 21). After passing immigration at the airport, you can shop for duty-free liquor.

Don't bring seeds or any plant material. Before you leave the airport, your luggage will go through an x-ray machine. Carry prescription drugs in their original containers. Anyone caught with illegal drugs can face 8 to 20 years in jail, and no bail.

Disabled travelers

Government efforts to accommodate disabled travelers has focused on accessible restrooms and hotel rooms, and wheelchair ramps into museums and public buildings, but most public buses cannot kneel or accommodate wheelchairs. Modern city hotels have elevators, but away from the city they don't exist. The best option is to take a specialized tour. Accessible Journeys (tel: 800-846-4537; www.disabilitytravel. com), based in Pennsylvania, organizes tours September through May.

E

Electricity

110 volts, 60-cycle current. Two- and three-prong flat plugs. Australian and European appliances need a two-prong adaptor and a 220-volt to 110-volt converter. Some major hotels have converters for guests.

Embassies and consulates

Australia: Honorary Consul; Edificio El Patio, Centro Corporativeo Plaza Roble, Escazú; tel: 2201-8700; aushonconsul. costarica@gmail.com
Canada: Embassy; Oficentro La Sábana, Building 5; tel: 2242-4400; www.costarica.gc.ca
Ireland: no Embassy or consulate in Costa Rica; nearest is in Mexico: tel: 52-55-5520 5803; www/dfa.ie/mexico
South Africa: Honorary Consul; 150 meters/yds west of entrance to Pacific Rail Terminal, Downtown; tel: 2222-1470; consuradricacr@gmail.com
UK: Embassy; Edificio Centro Colón, 11th floor; tel:2258-2025; www.gov. uk/government/world/costarica
US: Embassy; Calle 98, Via 104, Pavas; tel: 2519-2000; https://cr.usembassy. gov

Emergencies

Dial **911** for any emergency. Tourist police on bicycles patrol resort areas and are trained to help tourists in English, but most regular police will not speak English.

Etiquette

Ticos are noticeably friendly, hospitable, and helpful. Their penchant for politeness can be best summed up in their use of *regolarme* (make me a gift)

Celebrating La Virgen in Heredia

instead of *darme* (give me) when shopping or ordering in a restaurant.

People shake hands when first introduced. Women greet each other with a kiss on the cheek and another kiss on saying goodbye. Good friends and family, male and female, hug and kiss on the cheek. Children are taught to greet their elders with a kiss.

Excessive displays of affection in public are frowned upon. *No se permite escenas amorosas* (No public displays of affection) signs are posted in parks and swimming pools. However, such displays are becoming more common, as traditional inhibitions relax, especially among young people.

Elderly Costa Ricans are commonly addressed as *Don* (men) or *Doña* (women), followed by their first name.

There are no nudist beaches in the country and topless bathing is not acceptable. Off the beach, it's polite – and often required – to wear a cover-up or T-shirt, especially in a restaurant or in the street.

F

Festivals

The religious festivals during *Semana Santa* (Holy Week) are quite spectacular. Many towns celebrate Christ's passion with dramatic re-enactments on Good Friday and Easter Sunday. San Joaquín de Flores in Heredia has one of the most elaborate Good Friday processions, complete with Roman soldiers.

The Fiesta de los Diabilitos over New Year's in Térraba in the Southern Zone, celebrates Borucan culture, with masked dancers chasing out the Spanish conquistador devils.

In mid-January, the Folklore Festival in Santa Cruz, Guanacaste, features bullfights (bulls are teased, not killed), rodeos, folk dancing, and traditional marimba music.

H

Health

Inoculations

Unless you have recently visited a country where Yellow Fever is present, you do not require any inoculations to visit Costa Rica.

Healthcare and insurance

Many Costa Rican doctors trained in the US or Europe and speak English. In cases of emergency, you may not be charged if you visit a local clinic or hospital emergency room, but it's wise to have private health insurance to cover medical expenses and repatriation.

Pharmacies and hospitals

In San José, Clinica Biblica hospital (tel: 2522-1000; www.clinicabiblica.com) on the west side of town, provides excellent care and emergency services, with bilingual doctors and staff. In the western suburb of Escazú, next to Multiplaza, CIMA San José Hospital (tel: 2208-1000; www.hospitalcima.com) has modern facilities

Busy market in San José

and bilingual staff, too. Outside the metropolitan area, you'll have to rely on local clinics and hospitals.

If you have a dental emergency, call tel: 2208-8619 to reach the Advance Dental clinic at Hospital CIMA in Escazú.

You'll find *farmacias* (pharmacies) in every sizeable town, but few and far between in the countryside. Normal hours are Monday to Saturday 8am–8pm, but rarely open on Sundays. In San José, the Fischel pharmacy in San Pedro, behind the Office Depot (tel: 2253-1784), stays open till midnight.

Hours and holidays

Business hours are generally 8am–5pm, often with a lunch break from noon to 1pm. Stores are usually open Mon–Sat 9am–6/7pm. Large shopping malls typically open at 10 or 11am, but stay open late till 9 or 10pm, and all day Sunday. Grocery stores are also likely to be open on Sundays.

State banks usually open 8.30–5.30pm Monday to Friday. Private banks, such as Scotiabank, open around 9 or 10am. In San José, the Scotiabank branch behind the National Theatre is also open on Saturday.

Public holidays

Easter and Christmas/New Year's are the longest holidays. School is out from the first week of December till February. During *Semana Santa* (Holy Week), government offices, schools, and many businesses close for the entire week.

You cannot buy liquor in stores on Holy Thursday and Good Friday.

January 1 New Year's Day
March/April Holy Thursday
March/April Good Friday
April 11 Juan Santamaría Day
May 1 Labor Day
July 25 Guanacaste Annexation Day
August 2 Virgin of Los Angeles Day
August 15 Mother's Day
September 15 Independence Day
October 12 Meeting of the Cultures Day
December 25 Christmas Day

I

Internet facilities

You can still find a few Internet cafés in some resort towns, but Wi-Fi is widespread, except in remote or off-the-grid areas, where there are some expensive satellite connections.

If you have a Smart phone with data storage, you can buy pay-as-you-go SIM cards from Kolbi, Movistar, and Claro, the main providers across the country. Many upscale hotels offer free Wi-Fi but some charge for a connection.

Despite new communications towers across the country, there are still areas where there is no reception, especially in mountain areas and remote beaches.

L

LGBTQ travelers

Costa Rica has become a destination for LGBTQ visitors in San José and the

Time is precious

Manuel Antonio area, which have clusters of gay-only and gay-friendly hotels, restaurants, and bars. Outside those areas, discretion is the best policy. As with heterosexual couples, overt public displays of amorous affection are discouraged. For further information, check out www.costaricagaymap.com.

In Manuel Antonio pick up a free copy of the bi-monthly magazine *Playita Circuit* at gay-friendly outlets.

M

Media

Newspapers: the largest daily newspaper is *La Nación*, published in San José. *The Tico Times*, a valuable English-language source of local news and events, is available online (www.ticotimes.net). Another online source for local news and weather in English is *AM Costa Rica* (www.amcostarica.com). *The New York Times* is available in a few high-end supermarkets and hotel gift shops, but your best bet is online international news sources.

Radio and television: English-language radio stations include 107.5 FM, which plays classic rock throughout the day, with some news in English. Radio Dos (99.5 FM) has a morning and an evening broadcast in English and airs news in English every other hour, in between pop and rock classics.

Hotels with cable TV offer up to 70 channels, including 30 English-language channels. CNN and BBC International are usually available.

Money

ATMs

ATMs are proliferating but there are still remote areas without *cajeros automaticos*, so take sufficient cash if you are heading off the grid. You will find ATMs at the airport, at banks, in supermarkets, and in shopping malls. Any ATM with the Plus sign will accept any credit card that is tied to Mastercard or Visa.

Currency

The currency unit is the *colón* and there are bills of 1,000, 2,000, 5,000, 10,000, and 20,000 *colones*.

The exchange rate is tied to US dollars. In San José and most tourist areas, you can usually pay small amounts and tips with US dollars, but never coins. Hotels, stores, and restaurants rarely give as good an exchange rate as a bank.

Credit cards

Mastercard and Visa are widely accepted everywhere. American Express is accepted in San José and large hotels and businesses, but less so in the hinterlands. Discovery and Diner's Club have limited use here. Some small businesses charge an extra three to six percent if you pay by credit card.

Travelers' checks

You can cash travelers' checks at banks, providing you have your passport. Owing to some fraud issues, fewer businesses accept traveler's checks, so

San José's main post office

first check with any hotel or restaurant if you plan on paying with them.

Tipping and taxes

By law, hotels add 13 percent tax and service to every bill, while restaurants add a 10 percent service charge and 13 percent tax. Also by law, every menu is supposed to show prices including that whopping 23 percent tax and service, but many restaurant owners weasel out by adding, in small type at the bottom of the menu, 'Tax and service not included.'

Bellhops and taxi drivers should be tipped if they have been helpful.

Postal services

Correos de Costa Rica (www.correos. go.cr) has offices across San José and in large towns for buying stamps and sending mail. There are no mail boxes. In smaller locales, hotels can stamp and mail your letters and postcards.

Airmail between the US, Canada, or Europe should take about five days but the service can be notoriously slow. Stamps for postcards and letters to North America cost about $1.15; to Europe, $1.25; and to the Antipodes, $1.50. You can pay extra for registered letter service to ensure delivery.

For fast delivery of documents or packages, international courier services – FedEx, UPS, and DHL – operate here, based in the San José area. These companies also have a few pick-up services

across the country. Check websites for pickup points and prices.

Religion

The official religion is Roman Catholic, but church attendance is not robust, although religious processions are popular, especially around Easter. Marriages are civil affairs, as are divorces.

Evangelical Protestant churches are flourishing. There are also Jehovah's Witnesses, Anglican, Baptist, and Jewish congregations and Baha'i communities. In Monteverde, there's an established Quaker community.

Restrooms

There are few public restrooms and even fewer that you would want to use, so use amenities in a restaurant or bar (some roadside restaurants charge a small fee). Toilets are western style, but often lack seats and you need to bring your own toilet paper. Outside built-up areas, most plumbing cannot handle toilet paper, so it must be deposited in the bin provided.

Smoking

Smoking is banned in buses, taxis, trains, work places, public buildings, restaurants, bars, casinos, and national parks. Separate smoking areas are not allowed. Nevertheless, smoking is still popular, especially among young people.

Handing out religious leaflets

T

Telephones

Costa Rica's country code is 506 for the entire country. All numbers have eight digits.

To make an international call, dial 00 then the country code:

Australia: 61
Ireland: 353
New Zealand: 64
UK: 44
US and Canada: 1

Pay phones, few and far between, require a *tarjeta telefonica* (phone card), for both local or long-distance calls.

Cell phones

Your best bet is to buy a pre-paid SIM card with a local number. Kolbi, Movistar, Claro, and TuYo Movil, all with offices and selling points throughout the country, provide cell phone service using GSM technology (1800 MHz and 850 MHz).

If you have a Smartphone, SKYPE is your cheapest option for making international calls. Most hotels charge high rates for both local and international calls.

Time zones

Costa Rica is on North American Central Standard Time all year long, which means it is six hours behind GMT from November to March, and seven hours behind the rest of the year.

Tourist information

ICT, the Costa Rican Tourism Institute (www.visitcostarica.com), is the official source for tourist info. Pick up maps, bus schedules, and brochures at their desk in the baggage carousel area of Juan Santamaría Airport, or in their larger central San José office on the pedestrian walkway near the Plaza de la Cultura. It's open Mon–Fri 9am–noon and 1–5pm and inexplicably closed all weekend.

Outside San José, local tourist associations and hotels are the best sources for tour brochures and maps. For information on National Parks, visit: www.costarica-nationalparks.com.

Tours and guides

You can easily arrange day tours on the spot. The National Chamber of Tourism (CANATUR) lists accredited tour agencies on its website: www.canatur.org.

If you prefer to be independent, but want to spot wildlife, you need a naturalist guide. Most eco-lodges have resident guides, but if you want to hire a freelance guide, check their credentials. Bona fide guides are trained and certified by the National Apprentice Institute (INA).

Transportation

Getting there by air

Most international visitors arrive at Juan Santamaría Airport, 16km (10 miles) northwest of San José in the Central Valley. Some direct flights from Canada and the US also land at smaller Daniel

Oduber International Airport in Liberia, on the North Pacific side of the country.

Iberia, British Airways, and Air France now have direct flights from Madrid, London, and Paris respectively. Condor Airlines flies from Germany. Many UK travelers fly first to the US, then transfer via Newark, Atlanta, or Miami. Coming from the south Pacific, you can fly to Los Angeles, then connect directly to San José.

Public transportation

San José buses are cheap – around 75 cents – and cover the whole city, although very slowly due to traffic congestion. One of the most useful routes is the *Periférico*, which circles the city.

There's very limited train service during morning and afternoon rush hours, connecting San José to Heredia and Alajuela to the northwest and Cartago to the southeast. It's cheap – less than $1 – but can be very crowded.

Long-distance buses go almost everywhere in Costa Rica. They are inexpensive – less than $10 for most routes – but it's smart to book your ticket the day before to be sure of a seat. There's no central bus station; each bus terminal handles travel to a certain region.

For more comfort, air-conditioned minivans shuttle between San José hotels or the airport and most tourist areas and beaches on both coasts. Fares run between $35 and $60 per person; you can also buy money-saving passes for unlimited travel.

Gray Line (tel: 2220-2126; www.grayline costarica.com)

Interbus (tel: 4100-0888; www.inter busonline.com).

Taxis

Easy to spot, licensed and metered taxis are bright red and have rooftop taxi signs. In San José, you can hail them on the street, at taxi stands, or order by phone. Fares are inexpensive and, for two or more visitors, they're the most efficient way to get around. A taxi from the center to the western edge of town will cost about $5.

Make sure the *maría* (meter) is turned on when you set off. If you hire a taxi for the day or for a trip out of town, agree on the price beforehand. Taxis waiting outside hotels tend to charge higher prices.

Taxis Unidos tel: 2221-6865; www.taxi aeropuerto.com

Alfaro tel: 2221-8466; taxialfaro.com

Coopetaxi tel: 2235-9966

Uber operates in Costa Rica and fares are competitive, perhaps a little cheaper, but both kinds of taxis will end up in the same traffic jams. Avoid rush hours if you can.

Driving

Costa Rica is left-hand drive. In the Central Valley, roads are modern and relatively safe. Drivers, unfortunately, are not. Speeding, weaving, reckless overtaking, and aggressive truck drivers make defensive driving crucial. Unless you have nerves of steel, don't drive in downtown San José. Street signs are rare, traffic is dreadful, and parking problematic. If you do attempt it, use a GPS system and keep windows rolled up enough so no one can reach inside.

Vintage transportation

It's cheaper and easier to take a taxi from the airport to a San José hotel, and have your rental car delivered to your hotel. You'll be more relaxed and avoid the extra 12 percent tax at the airport.

Outside the Central Valley, driving is much calmer, more enjoyable and scenic. In the hinterlands there are still pot-holed dirt roads and a few rivers to ford, so if you're going to remote areas, high-clearance vehicles with four- or all-wheel drive are best.

Rules of the road: Seatbelts are compulsory; non-compliance is fined. Talking or texting on a cell phone while driving is punishable by a fine, too. Drink driving is defined as blood-alcohol levels of 0.075 percent, at which point you are heavily fined and your car is confiscated. Levels between 0.049 and 0.075 are considered 'pre-drunk,' and earn a fine. Speeding fines are also hefty.

Car rental: To rent a car, you need a valid license, passport, and credit card (not debit card or cash) to make a deposit. Deals may look good online, but check to make sure that the quoted rate includes compulsory liability and third-party damage insurance fees, which can almost double the rental cost. Your credit card may cover you for CDW (damage to your vehicle), but also bring along written proof that your home insurer covers you for liability.

The most reliable and widespread companies are:

Economy tel: 2299-2000, www.econo myrentacar.com

Alamo tel: 2242-7733, www.alamocos tarica.com

Avis tel: 2293-2222, www.avis.co.cr

Parking: Meter parking in San José requires figuring out a complicated meter machine, in Spanish. Better and safer to park in any of the lots for a set price, usually less than $2 an hour.

Outside the city, park in guarded lots if possible. You will often encounter self-employed *guardas* who will offer to keep an eye on your car for a tip.

Visas and passports

Citizens of the US, Canada, UK, Ireland, Australia, New Zealand, and South Africa need only a passport, valid for at least six months beyond your date of entry to Costa Rica. You can remain for 90 days.

Have a return ticket, since more and more airlines require proof that you will be leaving the country within 90 days. Make a photocopy of the identity page of your passport, along with the page showing your entrance stamp, and leave your passport locked safely in your hotel.

Weights and measures

Costa Rica uses the metric system.

Women travelers

Costa Rica is a fairly safe destination for women, especially if you travel in pairs or a group. Avoid walking alone at night or in a deserted area in towns or at the beach. Women should always sit in the back seat of a taxi and make a note of the driver's ID.

Slow down

LANGUAGE

Spanish is Costa Rica's principal language, so learn some phrases before you arrive, if only the simple courtesies: 'Good morning.' 'How are you?' 'I'm well, thanks.' These seemingly inconsequential phrases are an important part of daily life in Costa Rica. English is spoken by many people in San José and in the larger hotels, and one can always get by without Spanish; but if your idea of a good trip includes some contact with local people, then speaking a bit of Spanish is important.

The familiar 'tú' (you) is not used in Costa Rica, even with children. They often use an archaic form, 'vos.' The rules regarding the use of 'vos' are tricky and elude even advanced students of Spanish: best to stick with 'Usted,' which is always correct.

When walking in areas outside of San José, people passing on the street greet one another with 'Adiós,' or 'dios.' 'Hasta luego' is used to say 'goodbye.'

If someone asks, '¿Cómo está Usted?' it's always correct to reply, 'Muy bien, gracias a Dios' ('Very well, thanks to God') or 'Muy bien, por dicho' (Very well, fortunately') but you might want to try something a little more zippy and informal, such as: 'Pura vida' ('Great') or 'Con toda la pata' ('Terrific' – literally, 'with all the paw') or 'Tranquilo' ('Relaxed,' or 'cool').

Do not feed the monkeys!

I'm well, thanks **Muy bien, gracias**
And you? **¿Y Usted?**
Please **Por favor**
Thank you **Gracias**
No, thank you **No, gracias**
You're welcome **Con mucho gusto**
I am sorry **Lo siento**
Excuse me **Disculpe** (when apologizing). **Con permiso** (when leaving the table or passing in front of someone)
Yes **Sí**
No **No**
Do you speak English? **¿Habla Usted inglés?**
Do you understand me? **¿Me entiende?**
Just a moment, please **Un momentito, por favor**

Shopping and eating

What is the price? **¿Cuánto cuesta?** or **¿Cuánto es?**
It's too expensive **Es muy caro**
Can you give me a discount? **¿Puede darme un descuento?**
Do you have …? **¿Tiene Usted …?**
I will buy this **Voy a comprar esto**
Please bring me … **Tráigame por favor …**
coffee with milk **café con leche**
black coffee **café negro**
tea **té**
a beer **una cerveza**
cold water **agua fría**
a soft drink **una gaseosa**
the menu **el menú**
May I have the bill? **La cuenta, por favor**
[To get the attention of the waiter/waitress] **Disculpe Señor/ Señora/Señorita**
money **dinero** or **plata**

credit card **tarjeta de crédito**
tax **impuesto**

Getting around

Please call a taxi for me **Pídame un taxi, por favor**
How many kilometers is … from here? **¿Cuántos kilómetros hay de aquí a …?**
How long does it take to go there? **¿Cuánto se tarda en llegar?**
What will you charge to take me to …? **¿Cuánto cobra para llevarme a …?**
How much is a ticket to …? **¿Cuánto cuesta un billete a …?**
I want a ticket to … **Quiero un billete a …, por favor**
Where does this bus go? **¿Adónde va este bus?**
Stop (on a bus) **¡Parada!**
Please stop here **Pare aquí, por favor**
Please go straight ahead **Vaya recto, por favor**
right **a la derecha**
left **a la izquierda**
I'm going to … **Me voy a …**
bus stop **parada del bus**
reserved seat **asiento reservado**
reservation **reservación**

Driving

Fill it up, please **Lleno, por favor**
Please check the oil **Vea el aceite, por favor**
battery **la batería**
jack **un gato**
tow truck **una grúa**
mechanic **un mecánico**
tire **una llanta**

Reading in Parque Morazán

BOOKS AND FILM

Costa Rica has notable authors and poets writing in Spanish, but they are rarely known beyond the country's borders or translated into English. Most books of interest to English-speaking travelers cover natural history and life in Costa Rica, both past and present. The development of conservation policies, national parks, and eco-tourism are well covered.

Most books of interest to tourists are field guides to birds, butterflies, plants, and trees, along with coffee-table photography books.

On the big screen, Costa Rica most famously served as the backdrop for *Carnival in Costa Rica*, starring Celeste Holm and Cesar Romero, a frothy, 1947 Hollywood romance, portraying Costa Ricans as gaily laughing country folk riding in ox-carts and serenading señoritas in frilly blouses. The running joke in the movie is the confusion caused by the lack of proper addresses.

Aside from providing generic jungle backdrops to adventure movies, and a starring role in the 1960s surfing classic *The Endless Summer* nothing much happened cinematically until recently. Costa Rica is now bursting onto the Latin American movie scene, winning awards at film festivals, both in Latin America and in the US. Young Costa Rican directors, such as Hernán Jiménez, are building a home-grown and international audience for contemporary movies set in Costa Rica, employing local actors and technicians.

Books

Natural history

A Naturalist in Costa Rica, by Alexander F Skutch, early-20th-century adventures in the wilds of Costa Rica by the 'father' of neo-tropical ornithology.

The Monkey's Bridge, by David Rains Wallace, subtitled Mysteries of Evolution in Central America.

The Green Republic: A Conservation History of Costa Rica, by Sterling Evans. Focus is on conservation ethics.

Field guides

A Guide to the Birds of Costa Rica, by Alexander F Skutch, ill. by Gary F Stiles. The first, most comprehensive (and heaviest) guide to birds in Costa Rica.

The Birds of Costa Rica: A Field Guide, by Richard Garrigues, ill. by Robert Dean. Up-to-date bible for birders, compact, with maps and color plates.

A Guide to Tropical Plants of Costa Rica, by local botanist Willow Zuchowski.

Tropical Nature: Life and Death in the Rainforests of Central and South America, by Adrian Forsyth and Ken Miyata. Fascinating, easy-to-read essays on the wondrous ways of tropical rain forest ecology.

The Wildlife of Costa Rica: A Field Guide, by Fiona Reid, Twan Leenders, Jim Zook, Robert Dean. A compact, beautifully illustrated field guide to a

A young, avid reader　　　　　　*Location filming in Costa Rica*

wide range of wildlife, from insects to mammals, by local experts in each field.

Cell phone app
Birding Field Guides Costa Rica, created by Michael Mullin, Randall Ortega Chaves, Patrick O'Donnell. An invaluable aid to bird-watching with more than 890 images, plus vocalizations, range maps, GPS function, and ID assistance via e-mail. www.birdingfieldguides.com

E-book
How to See, Find and Identify Birds in Costa Rica, by expert birding guide Patrick O'Donnell. The most comprehensive guide available; download at http://birdingcraft.com/wordpress/wherehowfind-birds-in-costa-rica.

Photography
Costa Rica: National Parks, by Mario Boza. Bilingual picture book by one of the founders of the national park system.
Costa Rica: Wildlife of the National Parks and Reserves, by resident photographers Patricia and Michael Fogden.
Osa: Where the Rainforest Meets the Sea, by Roy Toft. Spectacular rain forest images by a BBC photographer.
The Painted Oxcart, by Michael Sims. A gorgeous, illustrated history of the Costa Rican oxcart.

Culture and history
The History of Costa Rica, by Iván Molina and Steven Palmer. Overview of the country's history.

The Costa Rican Indigenous People, by Rodrigo Salazar. Bilingual overview of the country's indigenous history.
Hostile Acts: US policy in Costa Rica in the 1980s, by Martha Honey. How Costa Rica's neutrality was compromised during Iran-Contra era and Nicaragua's Civil War.
The Ticos: Culture and Social Change in Costa Rica, by M, R and K Biesanz. Socio-anthropological analysis of Costa Rican society and culture.
What Happen', by Paula Palmer. A history of the Caribbean coast.

Literature and folk stories
Costa Rica: A Traveler's Literary Companion, by Barbara Ras, ed. English translation of short stories by Costa Rican authors.
Monkeys are Made of Chocolate and **Where Tapirs and Jaguars Once Roamed**, by Jack Ewing. Engaging and entertaining local tales by a long-time conservationist.

Film
Recent hits include:
A Ojos Cerrados, 2010. Elegiac, beautiful movie focusing on the strength of family ties in Costa Rica.
El Regreso, 2012. A native son returns from the US to readjust to the culture and family ties he thought he had left behind. Written, directed, and starring Hernán Jiménez, this film won best international feature at the 2011 New York Latino Film Festival.

ABOUT THIS BOOK

This *Explore Guide* has been produced by the editors of Insight Guides, whose books have set the standard for visual travel guides since 1970. With top-quality photography and authoritative recommendations, these guidebooks bring you the very best routes and itineraries in the world's most exciting destinations.

BEST ROUTES

The routes in the book provide something to suit all budgets, tastes and trip lengths. As well as covering the destination's many classic attractions, the itineraries track lesser-known sights. The routes embrace a range of interests, so whether you are an art fan, a gourmet, a history buff or have kids to entertain, you will find an option to suit.

We recommend reading the whole of a route before setting out. This should help you to familiarise yourself with it and enable you to plan where to stop for refreshments – options are shown in the 'Food and Drink' box at the end of each tour.

For our pick of the tours by theme, consult Recommended Routes for… (see pages 6–7).

INTRODUCTION

The routes are set in context by this introductory section, giving an overview of the destination to set the scene, plus background information on food and drink, shopping and more, while a succinct history timeline highlights the key events over the centuries.

DIRECTORY

Also supporting the routes is a Directory chapter, with a clearly organised A–Z of practical information, our pick of where to stay while you are there and select restaurant listings; these eateries complement the more low-key cafés and restaurants that feature within the routes and are intended to offer a wider choice for evening dining. Also included here are some nightlife listings, plus a handy language guide and our recommendations for books and films about the destination.

ABOUT THE AUTHORS

This book was written by Dorothy MacKinnon, a Canadian editor and writer who arrived in Costa Rica on an eco-tour 19 years ago, fell in love with the flora, fauna, and people of the country and stayed on. Along the way she has learned passable Spanish, racked up a birding list of close to 700 species and explored every inch of the country, writing travel articles for *The Tico Times* and updating guide books, including four Insight Guides to Costa Rica.

CONTACT THE EDITORS

We hope you find this Explore Guide useful, interesting and a pleasure to read. If you have any questions or feedback on the text, pictures or maps, please do let us know. If you have noticed any errors or outdated facts, or have suggestions for places to include on the routes, we would be delighted to hear from you. Please drop us an email at hello@insightguides.com. Thanks!

CREDITS

Explore Costa Rica
Editor: Carine Tracanelli
Author: Dorothy MacKinnon
Head of DTP and Pre-Press: Rebeka Davies
Picture Editor: Aude Vauconsant
Cartography: Carte
Photo credits: Alamy 4/5T, 6ML, 23, 36/37, 38, 40, 41L, 43, 44, 46, 53, 56, 61L, 60/61, 62/63, 85, 87L, 88/89, 91, 103, 106ML, 106/107T, 108, 109L, 108/109, 112/113, 114, 115, 117, 122/123, 124, 139L; Alex Robinson/ AWL Images Ltd 1; Bkamprath 137; Casa Botania 63L, 113L; Corbis 98/99; Corrie Wingate/Apa Publications 4ML, 4MR, 4MC, 6TL, 6MC, 6BC, 7T, 7MR, 7MR, 8MC, 8MR, 10, 11T, 10/11T, 12B, 12T, 13, 14B, 17, 19L, 25, 28ML, 28MC, 28MR, 28ML, 28/29T, 31L, 31, 32/33, 34, 35, 40/41, 64, 66/67, 75L, 77, 82/83, 84, 86, 92/93, 94, 98, 101, 102, 106MC, 106ML, 112, 125, 130, 134, 135, 138; Getty Images 8/9T, 10/11M, 14/15T, 18, 20/21, 26/27, 28MR, 45, 52, 58/59, 62, 76, 88, 116, 118/119, 129; Harmony restaurant 97; Iguana Lodge 106MC, 110/111, 127, 131; iStock 4MC, 4MR, 4ML, 8ML, 8MC, 8MR, 16, 18/19, 22, 24, 28MC, 30, 42, 50/51, 55, 60, 65, 68, 70, 72, 72/73, 74, 74/75, 78, 79, 80, 81, 86/87, 90, 95, 99L, 104/105, 106MR, 106MR, 126, 128, 132, 133, 136, 138/139; Joaquin Murillo/Orosí Lodge 48; John Borthwick 8ML; Le Tapir, Dantica cloud forest Lounge 54; Pawel Toczynski 57; Shutterstock 7M, 47L, 46/47, 49, 69, 71, 73L, 89L, 96, 100, 120/121
Cover credits: Nick Ledger/AWL Images (main) Shutterstock (bottom)

Printed by CTPS – China

First Edition 2018

DISTRIBUTION

UK, Ireland and Europe
Apa Publications (UK) Ltd
sales@insightguides.com
United States and Canada
Ingram Publisher Services
ips@ingramcontent.com
Australia and New Zealand
Woodslane
info@woodslane.com.au
Southeast Asia
Apa Publications (Singapore) Pte
singaporeoffice@insightguides.com
Worldwide
Apa Publications (UK) Ltd
sales@insightguides.com

SPECIAL SALES, CONTENT LICENSING AND COPUBLISHING

Insight Guides can be purchased in bulk quantities at discounted prices. We can create special editions, personalised jackets and corporate imprints tailored to your needs.
sales@insightguides.com
www.insightguides.biz

INDEX

MAP LEGEND

●	Start of tour	✈	Airport	❋	Viewpoint
→	Tour & route direction	✦	Airfield	∴	Ancient site
❶	Recommended sight	📖	Library	⚑	Beach
❷	Recommended restaurant/café	⚊	Statue/monument	⋒	Cave
★	Place of interest	✚†	Church		Park
❶	Tourist information	🎭	Theatre		Important building
–··–	Ferry route	✉	Main post office		Transport hub
		🚌	Main bus station		Urban area
		✚	Hospital		National park